W. O.

KU-602-624

GOVERNMENT OF EDUCATION

PENGUIN BOOKS

Penguin Books Ltd, Harmondsworth, Middlesex, England
Penguin Books Inc., 7110 Ambassador Road, Baltimore, Maryland 21207, U.S.A.
Penguin Books Australia Ltd, Ringwood, Victoria, Australia

—

First published 1965
Reprinted with revisions 1968
Reprinted with revisions 1971

—

—

Made and printed in Great Britain by
Cox & Wyman Ltd,
London, Reading and Fakenham
Set in Monotype Plantin

Contents

CHAPTER I

Who Should Govern Education?

WHO DECIDES?

As a by-product of the growing regard for education, there is today much more interest taken in the way it is governed and administered. Parents are less disposed to tolerate without protest conditions in school that seem to them unsatisfactory, or to accept without question decisions affecting the education of their children which they consider unjust or misguided. The social revolution, gathering momentum ever since the last world war, has stimulated this critical attitude; and there have been other factors that have tended to make parents more discriminating.

Many of them are better educated than the majority of parents were twenty or thirty years ago; they know more about schools and have views about how decisions are arrived at both within the school and by the education committee. Parent–teacher and other associations provide occasions for the discussion of educational problems, and Press and radio, finding there is a demand for it, do much to spread knowledge about the upbringing of children. The psychology of childhood and adolescence has, as a consequence, ardent exponents in innumerable homes; and, if sometimes sadly misunderstood, it has nevertheless a salutary influence. Health education has made parents more conscious of the ill effects of crowded, stuffy classrooms, and more and more appreciative of the advantages of schooldays spent in a light, airy, pleasant environment. Along with the greater knowledge of what a good education service should provide, there is a better understanding of how to secure improvement; and there is more militancy, and there are more angry young parents with zest for the fray. In many communities there are various societies, political and otherwise, that furnish abundant opportunities for ventilating grievances and organizing pressure.

Nothing in the administration of education in this country has generated quite so much heat as the allocation of pupils to secondary schools, colloquially known as 'the eleven-plus'. There was more aggressive hostility in the 1880s when compulsory education was first generally enforced, but the opposition then came mainly from parents with little or no regard for their children's well-being. The outcry aroused by the eleven-plus has been of a very different character: and, more often than not, it has emanated from disappointed parents deeply concerned about their child's education. They have protested vehemently because they are convinced that his prospects in life have been jeopardized unfairly by a system that seems to them flagrantly unjust. The eleven-plus agitations have frequently had strong popular support; and the Press, both local and national, has been ready to find space for a pretty full ventilation of the issues raised.

The controversies continue, but in a more temperate mood. It is now more widely realized that when Parliament in 1944 adopted the revolutionary policy of secondary education for all, it set local authorities a truly formidable task. They had to operate the new dispensation almost at once without the necessary school buildings, without adequate staff and other essentials. For years they had somehow to make do without being able to offer reasonable alternatives to the grammar school: and in some areas that is still the situation. Moreover they had to initiate this great reform with the whole educational service running at full pressure. Introducing universal secondary education in such circumstances was – to borrow Samuel Butler's saying about life – 'like playing a violin solo in public and learning the instrument as one goes on'.

During the years of disillusionment after 1944 frustrated parents were inclined to make the local authorities and their officers the main targets of their wrath. But that phase passed as the building programmes developed; and the various modifications in allocation procedures gradually made people more aware of the local authority's anxiety to ensure that, as far as possible, justice should be done. But some discontent is inevitable, for whatever the allocation procedure may be the competitive aspect cannot be eliminated. For the grammar school – or, in a comprehensive school, the grammar stream – is the normal key to social and economic advance, and it is not surprising, therefore, that, however attractive the alternatives may be, some parents feel aggrieved when their children are denied such a valued opportunity. 'It is known,' writes Professor Vernon, 'that roughly half the parents in the country desire this type of education, although Grammar School places are available only for some 20 per cent of children and for much smaller proportions in some areas. Parents realize that, in addition to the value of a thorough education as such, it provides the usual avenue to white-collar and professional jobs, and the chance of going to a University.'[1]

The battles fought about the eleven-plus and the publicity they received helped greatly to stimulate interest in the administration of education. Prior to 1944 it was usual to observe a polite reticence about the examination for special places in maintained grammar schools – the eleven-plus of those days. Its strictly confidential, hush-hush character was generally accepted, and the number of doubting parents was relatively few. But once 'secondary education for all' became the law of the land, disappointment was widespread: far too many young parents credulously believed that a grammar-school education or its equivalent would be available forthwith for all children of suitable age. Disillusioned, they protested, agitated, and probed, asking many questions.

Conversations on a bus or at a shopping centre at a time when the eleven-plus results were circulating resounded with educational jargon – secondary modern, I.Q., direct grant, age allowance, border-line, and so forth. A new relationship between parent and authority had begun, and barriers once deemed impassable began to disappear. Parents became more and more persistent and officials, anxious to ease the tension, were not loth to take advantage of opportunities to inform and explain. As a result of this dissemination of information about the mechanics of the eleven-plus one could by the 1950s assume at a parents' meeting a considerable background of knowledge about types of schools, selection procedures, and much else that was once the

1. Introduction to J. J. B. Dempster's *Selection for Secondary Education*, Methuen, 1954.

private stock-in-trade of education offices and common rooms.

The sceptical, distrustful attitude characteristic of the late 1940s faded away to be replaced by more intelligent and thoughtful criticism. Nowadays there is far less loose talk about the iniquities of 'they' and 'them'; for there is more awareness of the complexities of our educational system, and a realization that there are several spoons busy stirring the educational brew. When today there is local controversy about the eleven-plus or about types of school or about university entrance or any other serious issue, attention is focused not vaguely on 'them', but more often specifically on those deemed responsible for the particular policy under discussion: e.g. Curzon Street, County or Town Hall, school governors or head teacher.

Too frequently there is frustration and soreness because of difficulty in discovering where the responsibility lies; and this seems to be a serious weakness not only in the government of education but of our modern democracy generally. There were some interesting letters in *The Times* on this point shortly after the publication of the report of the Herbert Commission on Local Government in Greater London. One correspondent – a distinguished lawyer – maintained that the proposed reforms would not affect the crucial question of 'decision-making'. To abolish the L.C.C., create a Council for Greater London, and establish a number of Greater London Boroughs, as the Commission proposed, would in his opinion do no more than 'reshuffle the cards'. The job of decision-making, he declared, 'is done by chief officers, principals, and assistant secretaries'. 'A very few important members (not more than one tenth of the Council),' he added, 'exert varying forms of influence on those who decide.'

Another correspondent – a member of the L.C.C. – denied that the officers were 'the decision-makers'. Those who carried most weight, he contended, were those members who were able to give something like full-time service. 'Power,' he observed, 'flows naturally and inevitably into the hands of those who are able to make the work of the Council their first priority.' The sub-editor found an appropriate caption for the correspondence – 'Who makes the decisions?'[1] It is a question that many now ask,

1. *The Times*, 19, 26, and 27 March and 2 April 1962.

especially when aggrieved by some unpalatable pronouncement; but the answer is seldom as simple as the letters referred to suggest. Certainly in education, with its complicated and elaborate system, it is often most difficult to find out how this or that was decided. Graham Wallas, stimulated by his experience on the London School Board, devoted much of his time and thought to the intricacies of this problem of decision-making, and in his writings emphasizes the significance of human factors in the shaping of public affairs.[1]

A case study to determine how some local educational issue was decided could yield some interesting evidence, and historical research sometimes uncovers surprising detail about the tactics of combatants in educational battles long ago.[2] Now and again Olympians lighten their memoirs with strange disclosures. The austere H. A. L. Fisher – to give one example – tells how, from lack of parliamentary experience, he found some difficulty in steering his Education Bill of 1918 through its committee stages; and he describes how the veteran Labour leader, John Burns, came to his rescue with 'fatherly counsel', urging him not to make his speeches so interesting. 'Send them to sleep, Mr Fisher,' he said, 'send them to sleep.' And apparently Fisher was not unwilling, in so good a cause, to stoop to conquer.[3]

WHO SHOULD DECIDE?

Our ways of governing and administering education are likely to come under critical review during the next few years, and from several angles. The time is ripe for a general survey, for it is now twenty years since under the 1944 Education Act a Minister was created and given almost absolute power, subject to Parliament. It was Mr Butler's[4] expressed wish that the Minister should 'lead boldly' and there was at the time a strong feeling that some concentration of power at the centre was essential in order to promote a fairly even standard of educational provision throughout the whole country. Another view, widely held, was that in this

1. See *Human Nature in Politics, The Great Society, Social Judgment.*
2. See, for example, E. Eaglesham, *From School Board to Local Authority.*
3. *An Unfinished Autobiography*, p. 109.
4. Now Lord Butler of Saffron Walden.

age of planning it was vital to have a Minister empowered to control educational programmes on a national basis and able to determine priorities. There were, as one would expect, some fears expressed, both in Parliament and outside, that with so much authority the Minister might become an educational dictator. But Parliament showed that it was not unduly worried on that score by adding to the original Bill a clause (68) which authorizes the Minister to overrule any local authority, managers, or governors who 'have acted or are proposing to act unreasonably . . .'

'A despotic politician, appointed to be Minister, would find,' it has been said, 'in the 1944 Act all the powers he needed to twist the whole adminstration, local and central, to suit his purpose.'[1] The Minister's powers are certainly formidable, but successive occupants of the office have normally used their powers with moderation and, when they have seemed to use their weight unduly, there have always been the brakes of parliamentary criticism, the Press, and public opinion. It is significant that Sir William Alexander, with his unrivalled knowledge of the relationship of local education authorities with the Ministry, describes it as still a partnership, and one that works smoothly and with reasonable flexibility.[2] The Ministry holds much the same view. In 1950 it 'celebrated' the jubilee of a unified central department by publishing a survey of developments during the fifty years; and, in a preface, recorded with pride, as an outstanding achievement, 'the progressive partnership between the Central Department, the local education authorities, and the teachers'.[3] Since then it has exercised its authority increasingly but the sense of partnership has survived. 'The relationship between the Ministry and the authorities,' declared the then Parliamentary Secretary, addressing the 1962 Conference of the Association of Education Committees, 'has grown into a closer and more harmonious working partnership.'[4]

But in this partnership the Ministry is today very much the

1. Eaglesham, op. cit., p. 181.
2. *Education in England*, pp. 2–14.
3. *Education, 1900–1950*, Cmd 8244, H.M.S.O., 1951, p. 1.
4. *Education*, 29 June 1962, p. 1313.

dominant partner, and there is no desire to curb the Minister's powers from which the Ministry derives its strength. In pre-war days local authority representatives were never slow in remonstrating with the Board of Education if it seemed to be encroaching an inch beyond its narrow frontiers, but today there are few traces of this *laissez-faire* outlook. On the contrary, one often finds even in local authority circles a liking for strong leadership at the centre; and it comes as no surprise when a President of the Association of Education Committees asks in his presidential address: 'Should the Minister intervene more often and more decisively in the conduct of the service?'[1]

While there is little or no resentment of strong leadership by the Minister, many are conscious of the danger of educational circles becoming acclimatized to bureaucracy and accepting too readily, or as a matter of course, the gospel according to Curzon Street. One might expect those who think the Ministry too pervasive to invoke the local authority as the traditional counterpoise, but today the argument does not always follow that well-worn route. The talk is rather about our changed society and our new education, and leads on to the conclusion that our way of governing education is out-of-date and in need of radical reform. 'And more and more,' writes Professor Vaizey, 'there is a growing national debate about education. At the same time the teachers have become stronger and resent the power of local councillors and others to "interfere". Finally, the parents, as parents, are at last beginning to feel they should have choice – and choice means a say in what goes on in school. These three forces – the Ministry, the teachers, and the parents – represent a new balance, quite different from that laid down in the 1944 Act.'[2]

There are several other considerations that make changes in our ways of governing education almost inevitable. Consider, for example, the radical proposals of the Royal Commission on Local Government in Greater London: their effect on educational administration in this vast conurbation can hardly be anything but revolutionary. Doubtless, too, the reports of the various

1. *Education*, 29 June 1962, p. 1297.
2. *Education for Tomorrow*, Penguin Books, 1962, p. 98.

commissions with their proposals for the future of local government will lead to big changes in the structure and administration of local authorities. The Robbins Committee, too, urged drastic reconstruction, and their proposals are transforming the whole pattern of our system of higher education.

Yet another signpost pointing to change is local finance.[1] Expenditure on education grows every year, and the £1,500 million that L.E.A.s spend is likely to be doubled in the course of a decade. Under our present system the cost, after deduction of the comparatively small income from fees and endowments, is met partly from taxes and partly from local rates. Herbert Fisher, when President of the Board of Education, introduced a percentage grant system under which the central government contributed about 60 per cent, and the local authorities from their rates about 40 per cent of the net expenditure. Fisher did this partly in order to fortify the growing partnership between the Board of Education and local authorities, and undoubtedly it was an important factor in the development of a close and efficient relationship between central and local government.

This system was, however, terminated by the Local Government Act of 1958 under which the Government pays a block general grant to local authorities in respect of various local-government services, and places upon them the responsibility of deciding how much to spend on each service, including education. Their freedom to decide how much to spend on education is however a limited one; for there are numerous important statutory and other requirements which a local education authority is obliged to fulfil. Moreover the Government meets the full net cost of school meals and certain other big items of expenditure, but even so the amount of rate-borne expenditure, although less than formerly, is not far short of 40 per cent. The replacement of the percentage grant system by one of a block grant for various services was at the time bitterly opposed by educationalists on several grounds, but especially because it was feared that education – now much the largest item in the local budget – might

1. For a good discussion of 'The Finance of Education' see J. Vaizey, *The Costs of Education*, Allen & Unwin, 1958, Chapter 3.

suffer when Councils determine the annual apportionment of their resources in the light of advice tendered by their Finance Committees.

So far, however, education has not fared badly under block grant allocations but it cannot be said that all is well with the local financing of education. It has been said that the Englishman pays his taxes in sorrow but his rates in anger.[1] With the mounting cost of education the sum required from the ratepayer must under our present system increase year by year; and there is a growing realization that rates, which in effect are a tax payable by the occupier and based on the assessed value of property, are by no means an equitable form of taxation. 'That rates are a bad tax is undeniable,' writes one with the interests of education much at heart who has for long campaigned for a reform of local finance.

They are levied on rent which is a fixed charge, whereas income tax on business is only levied on profits, and an individual is allowed total or partial exemption if his income falls below certain amounts. In addition he can claim allowances for dependants. Rates, on the other hand, are levied on houses, shops and offices, regardless of any 'ability to pay'.[2]

Various alternative methods of financing local government have been proposed, including the suggestion that education should be financed entirely by the Exchequer with the local authority still responsible for its local administration. In that event the relationship between the Ministry and the local authority would become one of principal and agent and would be similar to that obtaining in the National Health Service. There is, however, a fairly widespread feeling that if the local authority does not make a substantial contribution to the cost of education from its own resources it will lose much of its independence and the Department will become even more powerful than it is today. The Department itself has made it clear that it has no desire to see a solution along such lines. 'The lack of resilience of the rates

1. A comment made by Lord Crewe, the Liberal statesman of Edwardian days.
2. Shena D. Simon, *A Century of City Government: Manchester 1838–1938*, Allen & Unwin, 1938, p. 157.

as a source of revenue,' it remarks in one of its annual reports, 'might suggest "bigger and better" Exchequer grants as a ready solution to the local problem. Such a solution should, however, be looked upon with a critical eye by all those who have at heart the preservation and development of the principle of responsible local government, which has been evolved in this country during the last hundred years and which underlies the present partnership in the administration of the public educational system. For it is the very essence of partnership that each partner should make a reasonable and proper contribution . . .; otherwise the relationship risks degeneration into one of principal and agent, paymaster and payee.'[1]

We are accustomed nowadays to moving fairly swiftly – and sometimes without much forethought – along the ringing grooves of change. If, as seems likely, our system of governing and administering education undergoes some rather drastic 'modernization', let us hope that there will first be adequate discussion and that in shaping reform the betterment of education will be the main objective. Most will agree that there is scope for some useful reconstruction, but there is much that is good in our present system: in our zeal for change we must resist the temptation to destroy what is well worth retaining. 'The passion for action,' wrote Bagehot with his customary shrewdness, 'is quite as ready to pull down as to build up; probably it is more ready, for the task is easier.'[2] An early advocate of 'government by popular discussion', he emphasized its value as a basis of a reforming policy; and it is to be hoped that those who care deeply about education will have, as they did in 1944, time and opportunity to examine critically and express views about any innovations under consideration.

THE INTERESTED PARTIES

'Train up a child the way he should go,' says the famous proverb, 'and when he is old, he will not depart from it.' But what way

1. *Education 1900–1950*, Report of Ministry of Education for 1950, H.M.S.O., 1951, p. 32.
2. *Physics and Politics*, Kegan Paul, 7th ed., 1885, p. 191.

should he go ? That is the crucial question, and it has been the cause of bitter controversy throughout history, and even bloodshed. For it is an issue about which people have held – and still hold – strong and divergent opinions. Education can influence so profoundly the thought and character of individuals and of nations that it matters greatly what its aims and principles are; and therefore it is all important how and by whom it is controlled.

Throughout western Europe education was the Church's responsibility during the Middle Ages, but after the Reformation control of education changed hands in several countries, and the idea of a national church, closely associated with the state, emerged. Later, Prussia provided a dramatic illustration of what bold leadership by the state could accomplish through education. Heavily defeated by Napoleon at Jena and humiliated in the Treaty of Tilsit (1807), she set to work at once to stage a recovery. Her statesmen were quick to realize that with the aid of education they could create a national spirit and produce citizens that would be a source of strength in peace and war. They developed a well organized educational system that played a vital part in bringing about the resurgence that led to victory in the Franco-Prussian War (1870–71), the unification of the German states, and the creation of the German Empire.

Subsequently, with an education responsive to national policy, Germany became a dominant industrial and military power, confident and ambitious. Japan provides another example of a country which with the help of a well-organized system of education was transformed by her rulers into a strong modern nation. During what is known as the Meiji period – 1868–1912 (Meiji means 'enlightened government') – she developed rapidly, and not least as a military power. Although Germany's expansionist dreams eventually resulted in two tragic world wars and untold human misery, the idea of a state-controlled system that the Prussian leaders developed so effectively has not lost its attraction. On the contrary, in this cold-war world the direction of education by the state is widely regarded as essential to national survival.

It is impossible to think effectively about the role of the state in education without being fairly clear about the meaning we attach to the word 'state'. It is unfortunately one of those ambiguous terms that lend themselves to differences of interpretation. One well-known definition maintains that

a modern state is generally a territorial nation, organized as a legal association by its own action in creating a constitution (such action being in some cases, as in Great Britain, a process along a line of time rather than an act at a point of time), and permanently acting as such an association, under that constitution, for the purpose of maintaining a scheme of legal rules defining and securing the rights and duties of its members.[1]

One of the merits of this definition is its emphasis on 'the constitution' as an important characteristic of the state: for in the government of education it matters a good deal, for example, whether the constitution (written or unwritten) is of a parliamentary or absolutist type. Some, however, may think this definition too legalistic and, like Karl Mannheim, prefer when thinking about the seat of authority to use the phrase 'body politic'. 'By body politic,' he said, 'we shall understand all groups and leaders who play an active role in the organization of society . . . Our concept comprises those political elements *par excellence* that concentrate in their hands administrative functions, military power, and social leadership.'[2]

In this country it took us a long time to accept the idea of state intervention, and until 1870 the Government limited its share in the provision of education to that of making small subsidies to certain voluntary religious bodies who provided and managed elementary schools. Prior to the passing of the 1870 Elementary Education Act there were stormy discussions both in and out of Parliament about the wisdom or otherwise of state intervention; for belief in *laissez-faire* was strong and there was intense controversy about religious education. The upshot was the curious compromise of 'the dual system', which, modified and developed, is still the law of the land. At the last big overhaul of our educational system in 1944, its dual character was critically examined. Most of the voluntary schools were in old buildings and, although the state had since 1902 borne the whole cost of

1. Ernest Barker, *Reflections on Government*, Oxford University Press, 1942, p. xiv.
2. *Freedom, Power and Democratic Planning*, 1951, p. 42. See on this point A. K. C. Ottaway, *Education and Society*, Routledge & Kegan Paul, 1953, pp. 53–7.

maintenance, the cost of improving the buildings fell wholly on the managers. It was a burden beyond their resources and without further financial aid they could not hope to bring their school buildings up to modern standards.

When framing the 1944 Act the Coalition Government of that time had, therefore, in effect to decide whether the dual system should continue and, if so, on what terms. As the Act shows, their decision briefly was that it should continue, that the voluntary schools should receive more state aid and, in return, accept more state control. An impression of how they came to this conclusion can be gleaned from this paragraph in the White Paper which outlined for the information of Parliament, prior to the presentation of the Bill, the various ways in which the Government proposed to recast the educational system.

Discussions carried on in recent months with the many interests concerned have satisfied the Government that there is a wide measure of agreement that voluntary schools should not be abolished but rather that they should be offered further financial assistance, accompanied by a corresponding extension of public control which will ensure the effective and economical organization and development of both primary and secondary education. It is believed that the view will generally be taken that in framing the proposals for such control the services of the churches to the community as pioneers in public education, as the protagonists of Christian teaching in schools and as having for many generations voluntarily spent large sums on the provision and upkeep of premises for this purpose, cannot justly be disregarded.[1]

In Scotland a much simpler solution of the religious question was arrived at. There a great educational landmark is the Education (Scotland) Act of 1872, which set up school boards on lines similar to those established in England and Wales in 1870. But, unlike the 1870 Act, the Scottish Act allowed denominational teaching in board schools, and the teaching given was usually Presbyterian in character. It also authorized grants to voluntary schools, but such schools were few. The next big landmark in the history of religious education in Scotland was the Education (Scotland) Act of 1918 which, as well as creating new local

1. *Educational Reconstruction*, Cmd 6458, H.M.S.O., 1943, paragraph 51.

education authorities, effected a remarkable religious concordat, wiping out all traces of a dual system.

It achieved this by transferring to the local education authorities all aided voluntary schools – some 500 Roman Catholic and a small number of Episcopal Church schools; but the transfer was subject to conditions designed to preserve their denominational character. It also enabled the local education authorities to provide new schools of this type, when necessary. As Bishop Brown, a leading Roman Catholic educationist observed:

The Catholics of Scotland got a settlement of the Education question better than any in the whole world. I say this advisedly because in no country are there schools maintained entirely from public funds, but with definite control of their religious character secured to the Church by law.[1]

Naturally many Roman Catholics desired a similar settlement for England and Wales, when the Education Act of 1944 was being framed. But, said the Government,

Conditions, history and tradition in this matter are, however, wholly unlike north and south of the Tweed. In Scotland there has never, whereas in this country there has always, been a ban on denominational religious instruction in provided schools. Here non-provided schools outnumber the publicly provided schools; in Scotland in 1918 nine tenths of the schools are publicly provided.[2]

When considering the difficult question of 'Who should decide?' we ought not, however, to restrict our attention to the two traditional powers – the state and the churches. Writing over thirty years ago Lord Russell listed four 'powers' as entitled to a share in the exercise of authority in education – the state, the church, the teacher, and the parent; and he added yet another, as an ironic challenge, the child, 'usually forgotten'.[3] Since then there have been great changes both in education and the attitude of society to it, which greatly strengthen the case for more participation by teachers in the government of education

1. *Through Windows of Memory*, Sands, 1946, p. 185.

2. *Educational Reconstruction*, paragraph 53. For details of the provisions for religious education in Scotland, see *Public Education in Scotland*, H.M.S.O., 1955, pp. 6, 16, and 17; and Education (Scotland) Act, 1962, clauses 15, 16, 21, and 22.

3. *Sceptical Essays*, Allen and Unwin, 1938, pp. 184–91.

and for more recognition of the importance of parental opinion.

Except in the university world, teachers in England and Wales play a singularly modest role in shaping policies that concern their vocation; and it will be surprising if, before long, they do not figure more prominently in educational affairs.[1] As well as provision for more consultation at the centre, it should not be difficult, having regard to the precedent of the regional hospital boards, to find much more room for teacher representation on bodies responsible for administering education, regionally and locally. At the beginning of this chapter reference was made to the growing interest of parents in education, and an impressive educational development of our time has been the establishment of parent–teacher associations, parents' associations and guilds. Their introduction has not always been welcome: there was inevitably the risk that they might do more harm than good. But such fears have seldom been justified, and usually such associations have proved of real benefit to the school. They can be valuable, too, as a stimulus of local interest, as a preventive of too mechanical administration, and, in the aggregate, as a protagonist of educational advance. For such reasons they deserve wholehearted encouragement, including that of representation on governing and managerial bodies. When the Education Act of 1944 was passed, many hoped that parents and teachers would participate freely on governing bodies. 'I suggest,' wrote Professor Dent at that time, 'that parents and teachers in particular should press for representation.'[2] But the hopes then expressed have not been realized.

The value of such bodies depends largely on the care exercised by local education authorities in the choice of governors and managers, when this is their responsibility. They are, for example, entirely responsible for the appointment of the governing bodies of all county secondary schools, and some of them fulfil this duty admirably. But in some areas the administration of this important statutory function is far from satisfactory. 'Unfortunately,'

---

1. In Scotland teachers and parents have had representatives on School Management Committees for many years.

2. *The Education Act 1944: Provisions, Possibilities, and some Problems,* University of London Press, 1944, p. 30.

writes one critic, 'it seems true that under some local authorities governing bodies are reduced to ineffectiveness. They exercise no real responsibility . . . Moreover, the composition of governing bodies (which is determined by the local authority) may be such as to exclude or reduce to a minimum that wise experience of education and of life which their members should possess, and to make each body of governors a replica in miniature of the full education committee, faithfully reproducing the same political divisions and dominance of power. Thus educational considerations are subordinated to politics and the potential value of governing bodies lost.'[1]

Time has taken most of the sting out of Lord Russell's quip about the child being 'usually forgotten'; for after he made that comment education became more and more child-centred. But there is at least one addition to his list of possible 'powers' that many would think appropriate. For today 'the local community' or 'neighbourhood' is often a staunch, but unrecognized, supporter of education; and in new urban areas especially the schools are frequently the first friendly focus of social life and, as such, as well as for the education they give the children, are warmly appreciated by people uprooted from their homes. In our estimate of the importance of the local community we have much to learn from the U.S.A., and a study of their ways of administering education will show that decentralization has good points as well as bad.

'From the very beginning,' it has been well said,

American education has been decentralized as regards control and financial support. The Federal Government in Washington has never exercised more than a very indirect influence on educational developments anywhere in the United States. But this is not all. There early developed within the states themselves a strong tradition of local community responsibility for the schools and a corresponding tradition of limited use of the powers of the state government in educational affairs. . . . No informed American is likely to argue that this situation is without disadvantages. It makes for unequal educational opportunity, difficulty of transfer from one school system to another, and creates other problems. Yet there is a very deep general conviction that local

1. F. W. Garforth, *Education and Social Purpose*, Oldbourne, 1962, p. 136.

control of education is highly desirable. It focuses responsibility where it is conceived to belong, in the people close to the children for whom education is being provided. It protects the schools from risk of domination by any central political power. It permits the adaptation of education to varying social needs, and to the range of personal needs represented by the particular children of particular communities.[1]

In our own country it should be possible, without diminishing the Secretary of State's right to lead or his power to maintain standards, to strengthen local participation in ways that would provide a much more broadly based counterpoise to Curzon Street than we have at present.

1. C. A. Richardson, Hélène Brulé, H. E. Snyder, *The Education of Teachers in England, France, and U.S.A.*, UNESCO, 1954, pp. 217–18.

CHAPTER 2

The Impact of History

'HISTORY,' said Benedetto Croce, 'is Experience'; and just as personal experience influences our character and outlook, so the past conditions to some extent the thought and practice of nations and institutions. We cannot, therefore, discuss our educational system to much purpose unless we have some regard to the history that has helped to shape it. But to trace the sources of some of our attitudes to education it is often necessary to look far beyond our own frontiers. For, like other European countries, some of our fellow-members of the Commonwealth, and the vast U.S.A., we are heirs of the western tradition in education and owe much to its influence as well as to factors more particularly of our own making. It is proposed, therefore, to draw attention in this chapter to some of the wider historical considerations, and in the next to take a closer look at the national background of our own complicated system.

FIRST THOUGHTS ABOUT DIRECTION AND CONTROL

Greece was the cradle of our western civilization, and her gifted citizens were the first to think profoundly about politics and about education. In all the literature about the government of education there are no books so stimulating as Plato's *Republic* and Aristotle's *Politics*, and in both of them 'politics' and 'education' are dealt with as inseparable, with training for citizenship a prime necessity. The Greeks lived in small city-states, of which Sparta and Athens were the most famous; and it is fascinating to study their approach to the question 'Who should decide?' and to read how Plato and Aristotle, by different arguments, both arrived at the same answer – the state. Their conclusion can be attributed partly to Greek secularity of outlook, but even more to the fact that these small communities were in constant danger both from enemies without and faction within. Theirs was, therefore, a kind of garrison existence, and on grounds of security they could not afford, as Athens discovered to her cost, to tolerate an unfettered individualism. For their very existence it was essential for them to have citizens imbued with a strong patriotic spirit, and both Plato and Aristotle stress the importance of training in citizenship. For them education was a top priority, and they believed that it should be carefully planned to produce the type of citizen needed for the service of the ideal states that they portrayed.

Each city-state had its distinctive character and, while Sparta and Athens both attached great importance to the education of their citizens, they differed widely in their educational methods and their objectives. The Spartans were a small minority of the population in their territory and, as the dominant class, had always to be strong enough to control the large subject majority. Besides, they had to be ready to defend their frontiers and repel any threat of invasion. 'The total energies of this ancient *Herren-volk*,' it has been aptly said, 'became concentrated on the con-servation of the state.'[1] Military efficiency was their constant aim, and the authority of the state was ruthlessly used to achieve it. Education was an essential part of this policy, and it was carefully planned for the purpose of breeding soldierly qualities, especially toughness, courage, and obedience; and there was great emphasis on physical fitness. The bleak austerity of the Spartan way of life is reflected in our use of the word 'Spartan'.

But it was not just austere: for it had some brutal features such as the practice of killing off by exposure babies with weak con-stitutions or some physical defect. Physique was all important, and newly born children were examined by judges appointed by the state to decide about their fitness. Boys who passed the test spent their childhood at home but from about seven years old to twelve they attended classes for physical training and athletics. They were then sent to boarding schools for more rigorous training. Corporal punishment was a main feature of the discipline, and it was imposed not only as a punishment

1. E. B. Castle, *Ancient Education and Today*, Penguin Books, 1961, p. 17.

but also as a method of conditioning boys to endure pain.

In other Greek states girls received no education except the domestic training that home life provides. But in Sparta, although they lived at home, great care was taken over their physical training. They had their own playing fields where, under strict discipline, they engaged in much the same athletic activities as their brothers. Motherhood was set before them as the supreme ideal, and Spartan women had a high reputation throughout the Greek world as good mothers and nurses. Their training was designed to strengthen their physique and at the same time make them good at child care so that they might grow up to bear and rear sturdy children and thus help to maintain a supply of brave, healthy citizens. In these various ways Sparta certainly succeeded in her principal aim of producing good and efficient soldiers. But the Spartans paid dearly for their narrow conception of education and of citizenship. 'The result was,' says Aristotle, 'that, so long as they were at war, all was well with them; but no sooner had they made their empire their own than their power began to decay, because they had not learnt to live a life of leisure nor acquired any more valuable discipline than that of war.'[1]

The Athenians had a very different attitude to education. Defence was important for them, also; but they sought to educate their boys for peace as well as for war. They had a wide curriculum designed to develop character, quicken the mind, and train the body, and in the later stages of their schooling they had opportunities of learning to appreciate various aspects of civic and cultural life – e.g. the civic assembly, the theatre, the law courts, and the art and architecture of their remarkable civilization. 'Surely,' it has been said, 'there never was an age that made a richer or more varied appeal to the adolescent. Here, if ever, life itself was the real educator.'[2] But Athenian society was exclusive, and this enlightening education was provided only for the sons of an upper class. These highly educated boys were destined to devote their lives to the service of the state, while professional and skilled and unskilled mechanical work was done by the poorer free-born citizens or by slaves.

1. *Politics* (Welldon's translation), II, 9.
2. W. Boyd, *History of Western Education*, Black, 6th ed., 1952, p. 20.

The view that trade and manual labour were degrading was a bad characteristic of Greek society, and unfortunately it was accepted by their leading thinkers. In an ideal state, said Aristotle, 'the citizen ought not to lead a mechanical or commercial life; for such life is ignoble and opposed to virtue'.[1] For this reason nothing resembling our commercial and technical education figures in the Athenian curriculum. Another serious weakness of Athenian society was its attitude to women. 'The glory of a woman,' said Pericles, is 'not to show more weakness than is natural to her sex.' No provision was made, therefore, outside the home for educating the daughters of the superior caste; and such training as they received was designed to give them an intelligent grasp of household problems.

Although good citizenship was a main objective of Athenian education, the educational system was not devised or controlled by the state. While the state prescribed certain regulations to which schools had to conform, their administration was left to private enterprise. Fees were charged and this, as Plato observed, resulted in the children of the well-to-do having the longest education. It should be noted, too, that while they laid great emphasis on the quality of citizenship, these freedom-loving Athenians looked to education to develop personality. Indeed one can almost summarize their educational aims in words that the Hadow Committee used to describe our own educational creed – 'social individuality'.

A remarkable feature of Athenian society was the education provided by the sophists, itinerant lecturers who helped to satisfy the thirst for discussion and argument. Some were inspiring teachers, and among them was Socrates (470–399 B.C.), one of the noblest minds of all time. Disliked by Athenian politicians, he was condemned to death, drinking the cup of hemlock – the customary form of execution – in the presence of devoted friends. But a great many of the sophists were nothing more than clever, facile talkers, who enjoyed discrediting conventional morality and repudiating the claims of patriotism and citizenship. We owe to them the word 'sophistry', and it provides a clue to the shallow type of adult education that some of them purveyed.

1. *Politics* (Welldon's translation), IV, 9

It appealed to young Athenians at a time when there was little communal discipline and a growing social instability. But the days of Athens as an independent state were numbered. Sparta triumphed over her in the Peloponnesian War that ended in 404 B.C. and then, as a result of constant wars between the city states, Philip of Macedon conquered them and his son, Alexander the Great, brought all Greece under his control.

PLATO AND ARISTOTLE

This brief outline of educational policy and practice in Sparta and Athens will give some idea of the background against which Plato and Aristotle did their thinking about the place of education in the ideal commonwealths that they respectively described. Plato (428–348 B.C.) was a disciple of Socrates, and his master's death at the hands of Athenian demagogues made him detest and despise mob rule. He grew up during the Peloponnesian War and lived at a time when the greatness of Athens, now weakened by class conflict and political strife, was drawing to a close. He was worried about the growth of irresponsible individualism and the tendency, encouraged by unwise sophists, to engage in futile controversy. We are only concerned here with his educational theory so far as it bears upon problems of school government, but no student of education can afford to disregard his thought about education as a whole with human goodness as the supreme aim, or to miss the opportunity of enjoying the nobility and the skill of his argument: 'the *Republic*,' said Rousseau, 'is the finest treatise on education ever written'.[1]

Athens and Sparta both contribute to his ideas about education and how it should be planned. From Athens he imbibed a respect for the individual and from Sparta, while hating its brutality, he derived his belief that education should be compulsory and that it should be controlled by the state. For him a close association of education with the state was essential, and it was one of his main contentions that the state depends for its character on the education which its citizens receive. 'It may be said to be Plato's aim,' notes Ernest Barker, 'to combine the curriculum of Athens

1. Plato's *Republic* (translated by H. D. P. Lee) is obtainable in Penguin Classics.

with the organization of Sparta, while informing it with a principle higher and wider than that of Sparta – the principle of justice – and continuing it to a later period of life, and into other and nobler studies, than Athens ever contemplated.'[1]

In the mild communism of Plato's utopia the state is supreme, with education as the dynamic force moulding the character of its citizens. 'So long,' he maintained, 'as the young generation is, and continues to be, well brought-up, our ship of state will have a fair voyage; otherwise the consequences are better left unspoken.'[2] Education is compulsory, girls are educated as well as boys, teachers (men and women) are paid by the state, great importance is attached to the environment of the school, there is state provision for adult education, and there are communal meals. There were features of this utopian state which aroused sharp criticism in Plato's day as they still do. Of these one was his proposal to abolish the family. Children were to be taken from their mothers soon after their birth and handed over to public nurses, and those that were defective were not be to reared. His object partly was to maintain a good stock of citizens, and partly to foster the unity of the city-state by avoiding its break-up into families. But, as Lowes Dickinson observes, 'there was another reason why Plato abolished the family. He desired to set women as free as possible to perform their equal part with men in the ordering of his society. He was the first and most thoroughgoing of feminists'.[3]

Another questionable feature of Plato's educational programme is that its benefits are restricted to a ruling class. The ordinary citizens receive no education other than the advantage of living and working in a well-ordered society. Plato's elaborately planned educational system was solely for the benefit of two groups called 'the Guardians' and was designed to produce a meritocracy of the highest quality. The lower group of this carefully chosen élite was to be given a training to equip it for military or administrative service, while the still more highly selected members of the upper group were to receive a long and exacting training with

---

1. *Political Thought of Plato and Aristotle*, p. 121.
2. *Laws*, 813.
3. *Plato and his Dialogues*, Penguin Books, 1947, p. 71.

the intention that when they reached the age of fifty or so they would have acquired the wisdom essential for service as one of the 'philosopher kings' of the ideal state.

Aristotle (384–322 B.C.), a pupil of Plato, was as sure as his master that the state should control education and was just as keen about the training of good citizens. But in his desire for a good type of citizen, he did not overlook the individual. On the contrary, he wanted by education to make good men: but, like Plato, he saw no necessity to distinguish between the good citizen and the good man. For in his ideal state to be a good citizen it was necessary to be a good man. The state should use education to achieve this objective. 'That the education of the young,' he observed, 'is a matter which has a paramount claim upon the attention of the legislator will not be disputed.' And, he added, this is 'one point' in regard to which the Spartans deserve praise; 'they devote a great deal of attention to the educational needs of their children, and their attention takes the form of action on the part of the State'.[1]

But while in agreement with Plato on these fundamental issues, he differs from him frequently and attacks especially his master's ruthless attitude to family life. Aristotle sees the state as an association of families, and emphasizes the value of the household as a social unit and as an important factor in education. In the family, he contends, the child is prepared for citizenship and the father, too, by his rule over the household, gains experience that should help him in discharging his responsibilities in public life.[2]

THE RELEVANCE OF GREEK THOUGHT AND EXPERIENCE

Some may feel that these events that happened and ideas that circulated in Greece more than 2,000 years ago can have little relevance to present-day problems in such a different world. It would, however, be a sad mistake to ignore the experience of the ancient world for such a reason: for 'modernity', it has been well said, 'is a question not of date but of outlook'.[3] And from our brief

1. *Politics* (Welldon's translation), V, 1.
2. *Politics*, II, 1–5.
3. Livingstone, *Some Tasks for Education*, Oxford University Press, 1946, p. 5.

glance at certain aspects of Greek education, it is clear that some of the problems that exercised these first thinkers about education were very like some of the problems that perplex us today. While that is one reason for studying Greek views about education, there is another almost as important. As pioneers, the Greeks started ideas that – for good or ill – have greatly influenced the development of western education; and we cannot hope to understand the educational systems of the western world if we ignore entirely the historical factors that helped to shape them.

There can, for example, be little doubt that the Greek belief in state control of education has had important consequences. For well over a thousand years the idea of a controlling state went into cold storage, but during the Renaissance it began to be active again, and with the growth of nation-states acquired momentum. The use of education to promote the revival of Prussia after her crushing defeat at Jena, already referred to in Chapter 1, provides perhaps the best example of the impact of Greek thought about state control of education upon modern statesmanship. It was no accident that Prussian policy reflected Greek thought and practice, for among the leaders of the revival were scholarly men well versed in the history and literature of Greece. This was especially true of Von Humboldt (1767–1835), who was first responsible for the programme of educational reconstruction.

At once a great scholar and a great man, he brought to his task fresh thoughts and generous ideals of life, inspired partly by acquaintance with the Kantian philosophy, partly by an enthusiastic study of the literature and institutions of ancient Greece.[1]

Nations today in this challenging world lead no less precarious an existence than did the city-states: the perils are different but certainly as menacing. This leads them, as it did the Greeks, to attach importance to education as a source of security and strength, and as a means of training citizens to be zealous in promoting the safety and well-being of the realm. This sense of danger was one of the factors that made the English people so ready to accept the strong dose of state direction and control injected into our educational system by the 1944 Education Act.

1. W. Boyd, *History of Western Civilization*, p. 336.

Explaining the Act to a Canadian audience at that time, Sir Fred Clarke emphasized the significance of the drastic change in the balance of power. 'The note of authority at the centre,' he said, 'is a new thing in English educational administration. The reasons for it in this critical age are easy enough to understand. Dangers abroad, pressure for greater equality at home, and unknown possibilities ahead are justification enough.'[1] The parallel with Greek attitudes is very close, and it is fair to surmise that as they drafted the Bill Lord Butler and his collaborators were conscious of it.

There are bad as well as good features in this Greek contribution to our educational traditions, and of these the contempt for mechanical occupations is important because of its prolonged influence on school organization and the curriculum. The harm done by it is described at length by Fitzgibbon Young in his learned appendix to the Spens Report. 'The distinction between liberal and illiberal education,' he observes, opening his argument, 'underlay all Greek thinking on educational values.'[2] So also did their concept of a divided society, and their view that trade and mechanical operations were degrading. 'It is right,' said Aristotle, expressing this attitude, 'to teach useful subjects that are indispensable but not such as have a degrading effect upon the learner by reducing him to the level of a mechanic.'[3] In this country we have been so much under the spell of this ancient view of technical education as inferior that only now are we according it a proper place in our system, and appreciating that the antithesis between a technical and a liberal education is fallacious.

THE IDEA OF AN ÉLITE (A DIGRESSION)

There is, however, nothing in the Greek legacy quite so relevant to the educational problems of our time as Plato's idea of selecting and training 'Guardians' as an élite of outstanding quality for leadership in the state. It is an idea that has played a big part in

1. *University of Toronto Quarterly*, Vol. XIV, No. 2, January 1945.
2. *Report of Consultative Committee on Secondary Education*, H.M.S.O., 1938, Appendix II.
3. *Politics* (Welldon's translation), V, 102.

the creation of our educational heritage, including the grammar school, the public school, and the university. 'Both in theory and practice,' says Lord James of Rusholme, 'those concerned with education in the past have always been conscious of the need to devote special consideration to those whose birth, or wealth, or ability marked them out as future leaders of the community. It is precisely the question which inspires a major part of almost the first, and certainly the greatest, of works on education, the *Republic*.'[1]

So active in current thought – e.g. 'the managerial revolution', 'the rise of the meritocracy', 'the Establishment', 'Gordonstoun' – is this idea of an élite that it may be well, at the risk of digressing, to insert here a brief comment on its evolution. The notion of educating a select few for leadership has been put into practice in various ways, e.g. the chivalric training of feudal society, schools during the Renaissance for children of particular families like that of Vittorino da Feltre (1378–1446) at Mantua, the courtly academies, and the kind of private tuition that Locke and others deemed 'necessary for a gentleman'. Of the considerable literature on the subject perhaps the book that follows Plato most closely is Sir Thomas Elyot's *The Governor* (1534) in which he outlines an education specially designed as a preparation for public life.

But while education for leadership has received attention through the centuries, it has acquired a new significance in modern times with the gradual transition of society towards a more democratic way of life. Who these 'top people' may be at any particular time or place depends on a variety of factors – political, social, economic. Consequently educators, who attach importance to the upbringing of an élite, have to adjust their theory and practice to the circumstances of their time and their country. A good example of such an adjustment is the one that we often refer to as the Public School Revival, when Dr Arnold (1795–1842) and a few other headmasters reformed their schools or established new ones, opening their doors to the sons of the new magnates created by the Industrial Revolution. With an emphasis on character-training they sought to prepare them

1. *Education and Democratic Leadership*, Harrap, 1951, p. 31.

for the responsibilities of leadership at home and overseas.

In these more democratic days there are aspects of Arnold's Rugby that invite criticism, but judged by the standards of their age what he and his fellow headmasters accomplished bears the marks of greatness, and has certainly had a profound influence on our educational ideals. 'When Thomas Arnold speaks of the education of the Christian gentleman in the public school of the nineteenth century, he has taken', it has been said, 'many of the virtues which we have seen appearing in the Middle Ages in the ideals of chivalry or in the notion of the responsible behaviour of the gentlemen of the sixteenth and seventeenth centuries, and has gathered them together in the special context of nine-teenth-century England. He had in mind an ideal which im-printed itself upon the the institution of the public school in such a way that it became an example for the grammar schools of England when they came into existence after 1902 when local education authorities were set up. Here is a case of the spread of an ideal which is in itself complex, having many origins, to groups within a society, very different from the groups with which the ideal was at first associated.'[1]

It was Matthew Arnold, one of Dr Arnold's nine children, who first saw this problem of leadership in a modern setting. We rightly think of him as notable as a poet and literary critic, but he was concurrently – as they say in the law courts – an H.M.I. for thirty-five years, and in that capacity visited schools not only in this country but also in several European countries. An educational prophet of the first rank, he diagnosed the needs of his time with subtlety and wisdom; and some of his reports, especially those comparing our educational system with those of other countries, have had a big influence on policy and, indeed, still have. ' Our society is probably destined to become much more democratic:' he wrote in one famous report, 'who or what will give a high tone to the nation then ? That is the grave question.'[2] 'Organize your secondary instruction' was one of his most

1. Mannheim and Stewart, *An Introduction to the Sociology of Education*, Routledge and Kegan Pau1, 1962, p. 43.

2. *Democratic Education* (Vol. II of *Complete Prose Works of Matthew Arnold*), edited by R. H. Super, University of Michigan Press, 1962, p. 18.

insistent pleas: for, in his view, the fate of our civilization depended on the quality of our education and on a good supply of enlightened leaders.

Robert Morant, one of the greatest of our educational administrators, held no less strongly the view that schools maintained by the state ought to contribute their quota of leaders. As Permanent Secretary of the Board of Education when the 1902 Education Act came into operation, he urged – nay, almost browbeat – the new local education authorities in his zeal to ensure that they took advantage of the powers, vested in them by the Act, to provide secondary education. He has been much criticized because regulations issued during his régime fostered only secondary schools of the grammar-school type but, be that as it may, the new grammar schools that he fathered so ardently are today one of our chief educational assets.

But soon after the Morant era the conception of secondary education began to broaden out. In 1922, Tawney, an honoured name in our educational story, wrote his famous pamphlet *Secondary Education for All*, and four years later came the first Hadow Report with its advocacy of 'modern' schools for older pupils not attending a grammar school. Then just before the outbreak of the Second World War came the Spens Report which with the subsequent Norwood Report sought to show how secondary education for all should be organized. 'Its solution to the problem', comments Mrs Olive Banks,

was in effect an attempt to secure that universal system of secondary education proper to a democratic society without sacrificing the older 'aristocratic' conception of the secondary school as a training ground for an intellectual élite. Thus, although every child would receive a secondary education in the particular school suited to his aptitudes and abilities, the potential professional and administrative classes would still be grouped together in what was once more to be known as the grammar school. By this means the traditional secondary school, now one of the three types of secondary education, could carry out with even greater efficiency its role in the selection and training of that aristocracy of intellect which was to replace an earlier aristocracy of birth.[1]

1. *Parity and Prestige in English Secondary Education*, Routledge and Kegan Paul, 1955, p. 6.

So this question of an élite, that Plato initiated, has become a central feature of the most controversial educational problem of our time – namely, how best to organize secondary education for all. If, like Plato, you believe strongly in government by an intellectual élite, it is natural for you to like a system which provides separate schools for pupils who possess more than average ability. Your attitude to this question will depend very largely on your vision of the future of our society. Britain, said Lord Hailsham (Mr Quintin Hogg) when, as Minister of Science, he opened a new science block at a grammar school, is moving from a society based on privilege and wealth to one based on technology and qualification. The democracy of the future would not be a drab mass of second-rate people in which distinction of intellect was decried as egg-headedness. 'It will,' he maintained, 'be, as now, a society governed by its graduates . . . and largely run by people who put public service in front of enjoyment, profit or leisure. The difference will be that the graduates will form a far higher proportion of the population and will be drawn from every possible social class.'[1]

One likely effect of secondary education for all is that we shall now rarely have instances of eminent leaders, like Ernest Bevin or Aneurin Bevan, surmounting the handicap of inadequate education and rising to the heights. All of outstanding ability will now be able to make their mark at school and university, and find their way early into the upper reaches of society. Clearly there is a danger that the practice of selecting potential graduates at an early age will foster the growth of a new kind of two-nation society – the intellectual élite on the one hand and those of lower intelligence on the other. Once again there will be the privileged few – but with intellectual prowess, and not birth or wealth, as the criterion: and the unprivileged many, of whom some will feel keenly a sense of injustice. 'Every selection of one is a rejection of many,' says Mr Michael Young in the introduction to his satirical *The Rise of the Meritocracy*. And he suggests 'that the clamouring throng who find the gates of higher education barred against them may turn against the social order by which they feel themselves condemned'.[2]

1. *The Times*, 24 November 1962.   2. Penguin Books, 1961, p. 15.

To many the idea of educating a chosen minority for leadership is abhorrent, and so is the practice of sorting children at an early age and allocating them to schools of different kinds. They do not want society to be under the perpetual sway of a highly educated hierarchy: different situations, they feel, call for different qualities of leadership, and they remind us that people will often come forward to take the lead in the differing spheres of life who, as children, did not show unusual ability.[1] Nor do they believe that potential leaders should be selected at an early stage, or that a high degree of intelligence is a more important attribute of leadership than some other qualities, e.g. character. Moreover they consider it important that leaders and led should have grown up together.

In a democratic society, where men and women cannot be dragooned, the organization and necessary discipline of industry must rest on goodwill. The good manager does not only comprehend administration and business; he understands how his employees, more or less skilled, think and feel. The professional man who despises 'the working classes', the labourer who thinks brainworkers enjoy soft overpaid jobs – both of these, with their neglect of common humanity, are a drag on the happiness and prosperity of a modern nation. School, by itself, cannot create social goodwill, but its influence to that end is not negligible.[2]

For such reasons many believe that at the secondary, as well as the primary, stage children, irrespective of their ability or aptitude, should be educated together in one comprehensive school. There those now judged fit for the grammar school should grow up alongside those now excluded, and provision should be made for the pupils in their forms and sets to pursue the studies for which they are most fitted. 'In a comprehensive school,' it is claimed, 'those, who in later life will follow many different callings, join together in games, in entertainments, in all that rich part of school life outside the routine of the classroom. At the very least this must be an influence for good.'[3]

Several of our comprehensive schools are now well established

1. See, for example, Marjorie Reeves, *Growing up in a Modern Society*, University of London Press, 1946, p. 46.
2. *Learning to Live*, The Labour Party, 1958, p. 32.   3. ibid., p. 32.

and it is becoming possible to form opinions about them based on experience. For a long time we had arguments for and against grounded on conjecture or on knowledge gleaned about American high schools. 'Owing to its allegiance to the people,' says Mr Kenneth Richmond in the course of a description of the comprehensive high school of the U.S.A., 'it believes that its first pledge is to the majority, and that once this duty has been carried out the minority of abler students will be quite capable of looking after their own interests. In other words, it is not particularly concerned to find and train any intellectual élite, preferring to think that the nation's future leaders will emerge of their own accord.'[1]

Many advocates of comprehensive schools in this country believed – and gladly – that they would be just as undifferentiating in this country, and just as indifferent to the special needs of the brainy élite. And the opponents of comprehensive schools – those who espoused warmly the cause of tripartism – made similar assumptions, alleging that in comprehensive schools gifted pupils would have a raw deal and that potential leaders would get little encouragement. For, they argued, the academically minded children would, except in huge schools, be too few to constitute a strong sixth form, offering an intellectual stimulus and a wide range of studies. But some of these schools have already confounded both their advocates and their critics; they classify and stream, and they cherish their bright pupils, being as keen about the quality of their sixth forms and their embryo 'Guardians' as any grammar school.

THE INFLUENCE OF ROME

'Captive Greece took captive her barbarian conquerors, and brought the arts to Rome.' In these famous words Horace epitomized the remarkable story of the diffusion of Greek culture. Alexander the Great, who in his youth had been tutored by Aristotle, with the aid of his Macedonian troops not only captured the city-states of Greece but also brought under his sway many great countries of the western orient. After his short reign

1. *Education in the U.S.A.*, Alvin Redman, 1954, p. 148.

his vast empire dissolved, but it had been his policy to plant Greek cities and towns in the territories that he conquered. And, although his empire vanished, the process of Hellenization – the spread of Greek civilization – that he had initiated continued irresistibly. Of the cities that he founded the most renowned was the one that bears his name – Alexandria – which he established in the Nile delta in 332 B.C. Much later – 146 B.C. – Greece became a Roman province, and by her many conquests Rome amassed an empire far greater than Alexander's. Greek culture penetrated far and wide, 'pouring,' as Cicero (106–43 B.C.) observed, 'in a great flood from Greece to Rome'.[1]

Although the Romans were as keen as the Greeks about training for citizenship, they did not until late in their history look to the state to accomplish it. For by tradition they were averse to state intervention in a service so closely related to the life of the family. 'Our ancestors,' said Cicero, 'held that there should be no fixed system laid down by law or set forth by authority or the same for all.'[2] And the reason for this attitude was that the traditional Roman answer to the question 'Who should decide ?' was emphatically not the state but the parent or, more precisely, the father.

It was a direct result of the Roman conception of the unlimited authority of the father (*patria potestas*). As the father had by law the absolute right of regulating the life of the son as he pleased, so he naturally had entire control of his education.[3]

But the mother also was a considerable influence in the life of the household, as the stories of the mothers of Coriolanus and the Gracchi remind us.

The father, as head of the family (*paterfamilias*) was vested with immense powers because the Romans 'had a profound impression of family unity, the conviction that every family was, and of right ought to be, one body, with one will and one executive'.[4] This exaltation of the father had its bad, as well as its good, features, and could involve brutality – the paterfamilias had the

1. *Epistles*, VIII, 14.
2. *De Republica*, IV, 3, 3.
3. A. S. Wilkins, *Roman Education*, Cambridge University Press, 1914, p. 56.
4. Hadley, *Introduction to Roman Law*, Appleton, New York, 1890, p. 121.

right to take the life of an unwanted child. But during their first five centuries, before Greek influence had wrought changes, the Romans looked to the home and the family to provide what they considered to be the essentials of a good education – character training, healthy upbringing, and a grounding in civic traditions.

A. S. Wilkins well describes the characteristic Roman view of education before Greek culture and ideals became fashionable:

If a boy grew up healthy and strong in mind and body, if he revered the gods, his parents and the laws and institutions of his country, if he was familiar with the traditional methods of agriculture, and had some knowledge of the way of conducting public business in times of peace and of serving in the field in time of war; if a girl learnt from her mother to be modest, virtuous and industrious, skilled in the duties of the household, this was all that was needed, that children should grow up what their parents would have them to be. There was no conception of, still less any desire for, any system of progressive culture. The usage of their ancestors (*mos maiorum*) set the standard at which the Romans aimed. What had been good enough for the fathers was good enough for the sons. It was the severest censure to say of a man that he had acted as his fathers would not have done (*contra morem maiorum*). And to maintain this tradition of conduct no system of teaching by outsiders was needed or desired; the discipline of the home could do all that was required. With the methods adopted the state did not in any way concern itself. Indirectly it did much to hold up a high standard of civic duty and devotion. But the manner in which this should be taught was left to the individual citizen. It has been noted as something of a paradox that while the Greeks were always disposed to look with favour on the interference of the state in questions of training and education, they never secured the same devotion and obedience to the state as were shown at Rome, where the lessons of patriotism were learnt in the home.[1]

The strict home discipline, characteristic of Roman education, is reflected in our country-house tradition; and some of the qualities of the *paterfamilias* live again in the middle-class Victorian 'pater', who in similar fashion often combined a grim severity with a kindly solicitude for the members of his family. One can find much to criticize in the *paterfamilias* idea but most will agree that the Roman emphasis on home training has been a salutary feature of our educational tradition.

1. *Roman Education*, p. 2.

This, however, was not the only contribution that the Romans made to thought about educational policy. Like Alexander, they planted their civilization wherever their legions came and conquered: and so the kind of education that they favoured found its way into many parts of their far-flung empire. In the days of the Republic they found it possible to rely largely on home training as the source of education, but with the growth of the empire education became more Greek, more elaborate, and more organized. Greek teachers (*grammatici*) set up schools with a curriculum consisting mainly of Latin and Greek: and later a type of higher education was provided at various centres in schools teaching rhetoric and philosophy. Students who could afford it were able to pursue their studies at a still higher level by attending courses at famous centres of learning, notably those in Athens, Alexandria, Constantinople, and Rome.

During the earlier phases of the empire, there was little intervention in educational affairs by the central government. But gradually and in various ways the state asserted itself. At first this took the form of imperial encouragement and, even, endowment: e.g. Vespasian endowed chairs in rhetoric at Rome, the famous Quintilian being the first occupant of the chair of Latin rhetoric. But in time patronage led to control, and later emperors intervened in the appointment and remuneration of teachers, and even restricted their number. In A.D. 425 an imperial edict made the government the sole education authority, and forbade teaching by unauthorized persons. From that date until comparatively modern times – certainly for well over a thousand years – the idea of the state as the seat of authority in education was forgotten.

Of all arguments for educational advance none is quite so effective as necessity: it accounts for much of the expansion in Britain today, especially in scientific and technical education. It also explains why the Roman state, contrary to tradition, assumed powers over education and why it encouraged the growth of higher education in the urban areas of the Empire. Confronted with the task of governing vast dominions, it had to establish an immense bureaucracy both at home and overseas; and its grammar schools, schools of rhetoric, and centres for advanced studies were developed to provide this urgently needed administrative man-power. 'Thus a great part of the state's interests in the schools,' observed Dr Edward D. Myers, 'arose from its need for civil servants. It recruited, now, from all social classes; it recruited very many of the graduates from the schools scattered all over the empire. The student who was proficient in either eloquence or the law could be almost certain of appointment to, and advancement in, the civil service. . . . As bureaucracies go, the Roman Empire was an extraordinarily efficient machine, and it was manned at the top by orators and barristers. It was thought that the old classical tradition did induce mental flexibility and clarity and that anyone whose mind had been developed in this way could, by on-the-job experience, learn all he needed to know about the management of practical affairs.'[1]

But this meritocracy – or 'exclusive *humanitas*', as it has been called – did not prevent the break-up of this mighty imperial structure and the triumphs of its barbarian adversaries. Britain was abandoned as early as 411, and there followed a gradual process of disintegration throughout the western empire. Schools closed their doors almost everywhere, and only in Italy did a few survive. 'Woe to our age,' wrote Gregory, Bishop of Tours (540–594), 'for the study of letters has died out among us.'

THE CHURCH TAKES OVER

Already we have seen two of 'the interested parties', listed in Chapter 1, in control of education – the state and the parent; now another 'interested party', the Church, takes the lead. At first its members suffered much persecution, but their anguish proved the truth of that famous saying of Tertullian's, 'the blood of the martyrs is the seed of the Church'; and from small beginnings it became by the fifth century a formidable power. In its earliest years Christianity won most of its converts among the poor and illiterate,[2] but gradually it attracted people from all grades of society, including leading citizens. Often well-educated, they wanted their children also to have the advantages of a good educa-

1. *Education in the Perspective of History*, New York, 1960, p. 112.
2. For example, see 1 Corinthians 1, 26.

tion. But under the Empire the only schools available were the grammar schools and the schools of rhetoric with their Graeco-Roman pagan culture. So they were confronted with one of those perplexing problems of conscience which members of minority movements sometimes have to resolve.

There were interesting differences of opinion on this debatable point among leading churchmen, some holding that it was wrong to submit Christian children to non-Christian influences, while others maintained that it was important that Christian children should receive a good education even though this involved attendance at a pagan school. Generally the latter view prevailed, and it is interesting to note that 'the Church appears to have been content that grammar and rhetoric schools should be entirely secular down to the fall of the Empire'.[1] It was, however, understood that Christian teaching would be given in Church and at home.

After much suffering and frustration Christianity succeeded in winning imperial recognition, and it was legalized by Constantine the Great in 313. This famous emperor influenced the course of history in other ways also. For it was he who founded a new imperial capital, that fine city which bears his name – Constantinople. This had profound consequences: for it hastened and intensified the division of the Empire into east and west. This cleavage led, in turn, to a similar partition of the Church and, indeed, of civilization. The west, centred in Rome, was mainly Latin-speaking, while the easterners, centred on Constantinople, for the most part spoke Greek. But the difference was not just a difference of language: 'the mass of Latin-speaking Christians and the mass of Greek-speaking Christians developed separate interests and modes of thought and feeling'.[2] In due course the western Church went its own independent way, and so did western educational practice with Latin dominant in the curriculum until fairly recent times.

Once Christianity had been legalized, the Church was able to build up an organization and hold councils to determine its policy with the result that 'when the Western Empire fell before the

1. C. Bigg, *The Church's Task under the Roman Empire*, Oxford University Press, 1905, p. 25.
2. Edwyn Bevan, *Christianity*, Oxford University Press, 1932, p. 135.

arms of the barbarian invaders, the Church had assumed in all essential respects the shape which she retained down to the time of the Reformation'.[1] It was, therefore, to some extent prepared for the momentous task that it had now to accomplish – that of rebuilding civilization in a Europe entering 'the Dark Ages'. From the first it recognized the importance of education, and used its organization effectively to establish and administer schools. The schools of these critical centuries were mainly of three kinds – monastic, episcopal, and parochial – and they were essentially vocational. For they were founded by the Church – then largely missionary in character – to meet its urgent need of an increasing supply of literate priests, monks, and nuns. But if limited in scope and purpose, this education was in striking contrast to the barbarity of the age and it provided the basis for future advance. We owe much to the zeal, courage, and enterprise of the churchmen of that dismal period; 'not a man in Europe who talks bravely against the Church,' Cardinal Newman once said, 'but owes it to the Church that he can talk at all'.

As well as the vocational needs of the Church, there was yet another reason why the curriculum of these early Christian schools was so restricted. A distinction was sharply drawn between sacred and secular studies, and for a long time any revival of classical learning was discouraged by those in authority. Gregory the Great (540–604), for example, deprecated teaching that included 'the idle vanities of worldly learning'. This hostility to the literature of Greece and Rome was strongest among those who had memories of the pagan atmosphere in the schools of Imperial Rome. In time, however,

the exigencies of biblical scholarship, or at least of a thorough understanding of the Latin language, conspired with individual temperament and acquired tastes to modify the effect of so thorough a condemnation of secular literature.[2]

Among the influences that led to a revival of learning was that of the Celtic Church, which flourished in Ireland, Wales, and other parts of Britain which invaders had not subdued. With a distinctive organization – largely monastic and independent of papal

1. C. Bigg, *The Church's Task under the Roman Empire*, p. 1.
2. Adamson, *A Short History of Education*, Cambridge University Press, 1919, p. 3.

control – it not only provided education for the young but also fostered study of the classical literature of Greece and Rome as well as a knowledge of the scriptures and of writings in the native language. 'For the gifted and scholarly,' it has been well said, 'the Irish monasteries of the time offered opportunities for learning unrivalled elsewhere.'[1] In the sixth century, missionaries of this Celtic branch of the Church founded monasteries in many places, including Iona in Scotland, Lindisfarne in England, St Gall (in Germany), and Bobbio (in Italy). Wherever they went they carried with them their classical learning and their concern for scholarly study. An interesting feature of this Celtic monasticism was its tutorial tradition with, as an important feature of its educational method, a close association of teacher and student.[2] After a long struggle this enterprising Church ultimately yielded to the growing power of the Church of Rome, accepting its authority and discipline.

Progress came when the new rulers were converted to Christianity, making cooperation between Church and state practicable. A good example of such cooperation was the founding of Charlemagne's Palace School in 781: the famous Alcuin was lured from York to preside over it, and he soon gathered around him a group of learned teachers. About a century later our own Alfred the Great was similarly promoting scholarship and, for that purpose, attracting scholarly men to his court from France, Germany, and, most learned of all, Asser from Wales. But setbacks were numerous, and there was no general advance in education until the cultural revival of the eleventh and twelfth centuries. Then there came some measure of stability and, in spite of clashes between pope and emperor, a general acceptance of the authority of the Church in the spheres of faith, morality, and education.

As life became more settled, the desire for organized study increased and students travelled far in pursuit of knowledge to places where there were teachers renowned for their learning. And the outcome of this zest for study was that remarkable medieval invention, the university. As we have seen, in the Graeco-Roman world there were several notable centres which students attended for advanced studies, especially rhetoric and philosophy; but the

1. Myers, *Education in the Perspective of History*, p. 225.   2. ibid.

idea of that corporate, self-governing institution that we call 'a university' we owe entirely to the creative genius of our medieval forefathers. For it is, as Dr J. B. Conant, the distinguished ex-President of Harvard, has said, a juridical and social concept of the Middle Ages: and, in essence, 'has remained unchanged' throughout its long history.[1]

The first universities began because in certain towns there were famous teachers who attracted students from near and far. Probably the earliest of these schools that could be regarded as 'a university' was one at Salerno in south Italy; there students came to study medicine because of the renown of certain physicians who lived there. Similarly students flocked to Bologna to study law, and to Paris which under the great Abelard and other famous teachers won renown as a centre of learning. Among the students in Paris were several Englishmen who had to leave in 1168 because of trouble – over the Becket affair – between the kings of France and England. Most of them migrated to Oxford and became the nucleus of its university, and in 1209 a migration of a group of students from Oxford to Cambridge led to the foundation of the university there. Other universities were founded in different parts of Europe and by 1500 there were some 80 recognized universities, varying in significance and size; and among the more recent foundations at that period were the three earliest Scottish universities – St Andrews (1411), Glasgow (1450), and Aberdeen (1494).

These pioneer universities had, without precedents to guide them, to deal with the now familiar problems of university life. Normally located in towns, their students often came into conflict with the townspeople, and the relationship of town and gown was a major issue for which rules had to be determined. There was also much controversy about how teachers should be appointed, and about the rights and duties of teachers and students. The statutes and regulations framed to deal with such questions and the traditions that emerged set a pattern of university administration that became customary throughout the western world. 'The legacy of these early medieval Western universities to the educa-

1. Quoted by T. L. Jarman in *Landmarks in the History of Education*, Cresset Press, 1951, p. 90, in his fascinating chapter on 'The Growth of Universities'.

tional ideals and standards of the modern West is enormous,' wrote a distinguished American scholar.

. . . The idea that teachers should be united into a corporate body, that teachers of different subjects should teach in the same place and be joined by a single institution, that an attempt should be made to have the body of teachers represent all human knowledge, that studies should be grouped into different faculties, that students should, after their preliminary training, confine themselves, at least partially, to one faculty or department – all this derives from the great twelfth and thirteenth-century academic foundations.[1]

Some of these new institutions had higher standards than others, and it soon became necessary to find a way of discriminating between those which deserved to rank as universities and those unworthy of such recognition. Certain criteria came to be accepted: e.g. the institution must have a number of 'masters', and it must teach not only the seven liberal arts[2] but also one or more of the higher studies of theology, law, and medicine. 'But,' says R. S. Rait, 'the title might still be adopted at will by ambitious schools',[3] and eventually it was agreed that university status with, as its hall-mark, the right to confer degrees should be restricted to institutions granted recognition by the pope, the emperor, or the king. (It may be worth recalling here, as an illustration of the influence of the past on present policies, that when the Percy Committee reported on Higher Technological Education in 1945, the Chairman (Lord Percy of Newcastle) contributed a postscript to the report to explain why, in his opinion, a College of Technology might be authorized to award diplomas but not degrees. 'In all civilized countries,' he observed, 'the power to award degrees was the distinguishing mark of a University.')

THE MEDIEVAL LEGACY

The idea of a university was probably the most valuable of the various contributions that our medieval ancestors made to our

1. Dr Edward D. Myers, *Education in the Perspective of History*, New York, Harper, 1960, p. 220.
2. The Liberal Arts were divided into two groups: the *Trivium:* grammar, rhetoric, and dialectic; and the *Quadrivium:* arithmetic, geometry, astronomy, music.
3. *Life in the Mediaeval University*, Cambridge University Press, 1918, p. 8.

ways of providing and administering education. In England we owe them a special debt because here they also bequeathed to us the idea of the college system which 'though it had originated in Paris, became in the end the unique characteristic of the two English universities'.[1] 'The rapid growth of the college system,' Trevelyan says, 'brought about an improvement in morals and discipline, and a civilizing of academic life, for which later generations of Englishmen stand deeply in debt to the Oxford and Cambridge of the late medieval period.' William of Wykeham used the same corporate idea when he founded Winchester, providing it with statutes modelled on those of Merton and Queen's Colleges, Oxford, and on those of the College of Navarre in Paris.

Winchester with its warden and fellows was an independent corporation – a school existing for itself – though closely allied with New College, its sister house in Oxford. New College elected the Warden of Winchester, and fellows of Winchester were to be, for preference, fellows of New College. The seventy scholars at Winchester were to lead a community life.[2]

As to curriculum, it was to be a grammar school: for, declared its founder, 'grammar is the foundation, gate, and source of all the liberal arts.' Eton, founded by Henry VI in 1440, with its governing body of provost and fellows was a similar conception of a grammar school conducted as a resident, self-governing, and corporate society.

It may well be that we have something to learn in our organization of education from the medieval conception of 'a society'. Medieval thinkers were much influenced by Roman law, a knowledge of which spread far and wide from famous legal schools, especially Bologna. *Societas* was a basic feature of Roman law, the term implying an association of partners for the benefit of all concerned. It was natural, therefore, in the Middle Ages to think of a college or school as a *societas*, and to attribute to it a corporate identity. 'The Romano-Canonical Theory of Corporations,' wrote Gierke, 'although it decomposed and radically transmuted

1. G. M. Trevelyan, *English Social History*, Longmans, 1944, pp. 54–5.
2. T. L. Jarman, *Landmarks in the History of Education*, pp. 113–14.

the German notion of the autonomous life of communities and fellowships, always ensured to the non-sovereign community a certain "independent life" of its own, a sphere of rights within the domain of public law, a sphere that belonged to it merely because it was a community.'[1]

Many schools, however, while enjoying a good measure of independence, tied their own hands with meticulous ordinances and regulations, laying down the law about such matters as teachers' qualifications, duties, and conduct or about attendance at church and religious observances.[2] Universities were similarly addicted to regulating the community life, and the students even enjoyed charting their course of studies in great detail. 'One cannot,' wrote Spencer Leeson, 'imagine a medieval student without a scheme for his studies as well as a scheme for the world.'[3] But these foibles do not detract from the value of the corporate society as a device of government.

The use of this device was, of course, not restricted to the administration of schools and colleges. It played a big part in the development of local government, and in the growth of various social groups. 'Our country, above all countries,' observes Ernest Barker, 'has been a paradise of guilds and clubs. In our Middle Ages there was an abundance of merchant guilds, craft guilds, religious guilds; there were Inns of Court for the lawyers and free universities, which were guilds of masters, or scholars, or both, for the body of students. The same sort of abundance marks our modern history. The law of trust, under cover of which property can be held by trustees for a voluntary organization which cannot or does not itself hold property, had cooperated with our native tendency to produce a network of social groups.'[4]

This device of government could with advantage be used in the educational field more freely in these days when the state is sometimes oppressively dominant. The Department of Education could profitably leave more scope for initiative and enterprise to local

1. Gierke, *Political Theories of the Middle Age*, translated with introduction by F. W. Maitland, Cambridge University Press, 1913, p. 98.
2. For examples see A. F. Leach, *Educational Charters*, Cambridge University Press, 1911.
3. *Christian Education*, Longmans, 1947, p. 58.
4. *National Character*, Methuen, 1927, pp. 274-5.

education authorities which, in turn, could usefully share their responsibilities more liberally with governing bodies, carefully chosen for their purpose. Those who shape our educational policy might on this last point learn a good deal by reflecting on the ways in which medieval administration, while operating within an authoritarian framework, contrived to allow their institutions a wide measure of autonomy. 'A free community,' wrote A. J. Carlyle, explaining the kind of freedom that many medieval institutions enjoyed, 'was one which lived by its own law, and under the terms of the supremacy of the community itself, not only in its own law, but in its control over all matters which concerned its life.'[1] Such is the freedom that William of Wykeham ensured for his Winchester; and there is no good reason why schools within the state system should not be administered in much the same way.

Throughout the Middle Ages western Christendom was undivided, and the one Church provided the authoritarian framework within which education and other social services developed. Like Britain today, the Church had a three-tier system for administering education. We have the Department of Education, the local authority, and governing bodies: the Church had its central government, its diocesan organization, and a governing body associated with the school either separately or in connexion with cathedral, abbey, or guild. Much of the policy at the centre was shaped by councils. For example, the important Council of Westminster of 1102, over which Anselm presided, had several educational items on its agenda – e.g. how to ensure that no one taught who was not deemed suitable, and how to prevent the setting up of free-lance or unauthorized schools. The diocesan organization has been likened to a regional inspectorate with the bishop (or the chancellor) acting as chief inspector of schools, and the archdeacon and other dignitaries as inspectors. As for the third tier, the local administrators or governors, they, as we have seen, enjoyed a wide measure of freedom. There were often too many regulations, but most of them were of the school's own making; and as for inspection, they were, of course, subject to visitations but bishops and their emissaries had wide areas to

1. *Political Liberty*, Oxford University Press, 1941, p. 21.

traverse, and travel on unmade roads must have been a formidable obstacle to regular inspection.

The ecclesiastical authorities were particularly concerned to ensure that all teachers were loyal to the Church and, from its standpoint, doctrinally sound. For this purpose they made much use of a powerful weapon, the bishop's licence to teach, and they forbade anyone to teach who did not possess it. This weapon was wielded vigorously during periods of political and religious ferment like that in the days of Wycliffe: and, as we shall see, it continued to be used energetically by the Anglican church after the Reformation. McCarthyism, as we now sometimes call inquisitional practices of this kind, has, alas, a long history in the educational field. At first, while still in its missionary or pioneer phase, the Church must have found the administration of education comparatively simple. But the scholastic scene did not stand still, and, soon, schools set up to serve the immediate vocational needs of cathedrals and monasteries developed to become grammar schools. An important figure in the task of administration was the *scholasticus* or chancellor, a dignitary of the cathedral or collegiate church; functioning more or less as the diocesan education officer, it often fell to him to issue or withhold the bishop's licence to teach.

A factor of great significance for the future was this evolution of grammar schools and it was a central feature of church policy from the eleventh century onwards. During the famous papacy of Gregory VII (Pope, 1073–86) all bishops were asked to see that 'the art of grammar was taught in their churches', and a Lateran Council in 1215 decreed that grammar-school masters should be appointed 'not only in the cathedral church but also in others that can afford it'. Churches, chantries, and monasteries were, however, not the only providers of grammar schools: guilds and hospitals (often guest-houses for travellers) also provided them. It has been estimated that at the close of the Middle Ages there were in England and Wales about 400 grammar schools, for a population of some $2\frac{1}{2}$ million. They were mostly small, but numerically in proportion to the population it was a better provision than we had during the first half of the nineteenth century.

Medieval grammar schools liked to have intelligent pupils.

'Clever boys of humble origin,' says Trevelyan, 'rose through such schools to be clerks and priests, for the Church was still the career of ambition most easily open to the poor.'[1] The growth of universities stimulated the provision of such schools, and encouraged the preference for pupils of ability, while the need for Latin, not only for worship and study, but also for various professional and administrative duties made the training of an intellectual élite once again an important educational function. While the few thus had the advantage of a grammar-school education, the many were more or less illiterate: for 'no attempt was made to teach reading and writing to the mass of the people'.[2] But from references in the decrees of councils and in episcopal charges it is clear that parish priests were expected to teach the boys and girls of their flocks. Such teaching may often have amounted to no more than the catechizing of the children, but it was not without historical significance. For from it developed the idea of the village school, closely associated with the parish church.[3]

Discipline was harsh, but there was a new attitude to human life based on the Christian religion and, through the Old Testament, on the Jewish regard for the family and for childhood. The practice prevalent in antiquity of exposing unfit babies to die passed into oblivion. 'It was,' observes Professor Castle, 'this Hebrew view of the sanctity of human life, passing through the medium of Christianity into the Roman world, that finally destroyed the monstrous evil of infanticide.'[4] For similar reasons the attitude to people suffering from mental or physical disability changed, and hospices for the blind were established during the medieval period.[5] But it has taken a cruelly long time for these humane principles to gain general acceptance: and one must admit that until recent times childhood had a pretty raw deal and it is, alas, true that schools for the handicapped were not established in Britain until the second half of the eighteenth century.

1. *English Social History*, p. 52.
2. Trevelyan, *English Social History*, p. 52.
3. See Myers, *Education in the Perspective of History*, p. 210, and H. I. Marrou, *A History of Education in Antiquity*, Sheed and Ward, 1956, p. 336.
4. *Ancient Education and Today*, p. 169.
5. D. G. Pritchard, *Education and the Handicapped*, 1760–1960, Routledge and Kegan Paul, 1963, pp. 1, 2.

The cult of chivalry was one of the most interesting aspects of medieval education. Designed for boys of high rank in the gradations of feudalism, it was intended to fit them for leadership in war and peace as worthy knights or efficient managers of estates. The education, an aristocratic alternative to that of the grammar school and university, had an outdoor emphasis: the page was, according to theory, grounded not in 'the seven liberal arts' of the academic culture but in 'the seven free arts' – riding, swimming, boxing, hawking, archery, chess, and verse-making. Closely associated with the Church, chivalry had admirable ideals – 'truth and honour, freedom and courtesy' – though it must have been difficult always to live up to them. It lost its attraction when feudalism declined and with it the need for an appropriate élite; but some of its aspirations and, also, some of its methods have become part of our educational tradition. They are prominent today in such enterprises as the Boy Scout and the Outward Bound movements, and also in Gordonstoun.

We owe the superb architecture and craftmanship of the Middle Ages to yet another way of providing education – the system of apprenticeships under the aegis of the guilds. 'The guilds,' it has been said, 'were the societies which built up and expressed the professional ideals of the merchants and craftsmen, in a way parallel to the chivalric ideals which served the noblemen. The system of apprenticeship carried with it the neccessity for sound elementary knowledge and a growing mastery of craft with the recognition that there were standards of workmanship and integrity in membership of a guild. Here again the place and importance of the Church and of Christian ideals can be seen.'[1]

The Church, indeed, dominated all fields of education. '*La doctrine et information des infants est chose spirituelle*', declared an old Norman precept; and although western Christendom split asunder at the Reformation, the notion that education should be administered by the Church survived. It not only survived: it persisted, and in this country until 1870 all public education was under the control of a religious body – Anglican, Nonconformist, Roman Catholic, or Jewish.

1. Mannheim and Stewart, *An Introduction to the Sociology of Education*, p. 37.

CHAPTER 3

From Conflict to Compromise

THE BREAK-UP OF WESTERN CHRISTENDOM

OUR own times are sometimes said to resemble those of the Renaissance, that fascinating period in the history of Europe when the Middle Ages drew to a close and the modern world began. Certainly the wind of change blew strongly then as it does today: there were remarkable inventions, good and bad, for example, printing and gunpowder; great discoveries, including the momentous discovery of America; much new knowledge, a growth of nationalism, and a questioning spirit. Their humanism, based largely on revived study of Latin and Greek authors, and their delight in literature and the arts may be said to have its counterpart today in the growing enthusiasm in the realms of science and technology. They had, like us, a questioning spirit – 'an immediate and fresh look at man and human experience may be said to sum up the Revival'[1] – and we certainly share their predilection for challenging conventional attitudes and contesting time-honoured beliefs.

It cannot be said, however, that the Renaissance made a notable contribution to educational advance within universities and schools. There was much theory, and there were some thrilling instances of individual enterprise – for example, the House of Joy that Vittorino da Feltre (1378–1446) established at Mantua; but schools generally did not show much inclination to change their ways. Greek crept into the curriculum: but neither in Latin nor Greek were the authors studied in relation to their human background. 'Mere style or form ... became the aim; and then finally, alas, grammar.'[2] Unfortunately this narrow curriculum

1. S. S. Laurie, *Educational Opinion from the Renaissance*, Cambridge University Press, 1905, p. 6.
2. ibid., p. 66.

was usual in grammar schools until the beginning of this century. Outside the schools the educational situation was, also, depressing: and in northern Europe, especially, education suffered severely as a result of those divisive tendencies that culminated in the break-up of Christendom at the Reformation.

'The Renaissance and Reformation,' observed Sir Cyril Norwood, 'were both disintegrating influences. . . . It was the Reformation which in this country dealt the hardest blow to education. It broke up the unity of the nation. The Catholics were outlawed and persecuted, and the Protestants broke into sects. Many schools were plundered and destroyed, and a spirit of self-seeking, or private profit to be made at the expense of the public benefit, was let loose. By the end of the reign of Elizabeth, many of the schools were refounded, but in a different spirit, with smaller resources, and with less opportunity. They were for one class, the sons of the members of the Established Church. There was no access for the sons of Catholics or Nonconformists. The old ideals were lost sight of, and the seventeenth and eighteenth centuries are a dark period in the history of English education.'[1]

In countries ceasing to accept the supremacy of the Pope in religious affairs, it was necessary to come to some decision how religion should be governed. The idea of there being only one Church in a country, and of its having a wide range of responsibilities, still prevailed.

Protestants, not less than Catholics, emphasized the idea of Church-civilization, in which all departments of life, the State and society, education and science, law, commerce and industry were to be regulated in accordance with the law of God.[2]

But what Church ? The German states adopted as their answer to this question the principle that the religion of each state should be that of its ruler – *cujus regio, ejus religio.*

The Reformation was, however, a movement of many influences, operating in different ways in the countries in which it triumphed. Nowhere did it benefit education more effectively than in Scotland. There Calvinism found a divided country, in

1. *The English Tradition of Education*, Murray, 1929, p. 13.
2. R. H. Tawney, *Religion and the Rise of Capitalism*, Penguin Books, 1938, p. 94.

which the clergy, the burghs, the feudal lords, and the crown were all at variance. After a long, bitter struggle the Calvinistic presbyterians gained the mastery, and presently discord gave way to a sense of unity. 'The Scottish people became at last a single nation: but the essence of their nationality was a national form of religion.'[1]

John Calvin (1509–69) had himself taught in Sturm's gymnasium in Strasburg and later founded a college in Geneva. His educational principles were adopted in countries where his religious doctrines took root, and especially in Scotland under the dynamic influence of John Knox. Knox's *First Book of Discipline* (1560) included a scheme which provided that every town should have a school and every parish a schoolmaster; and that the children of all, whether rich or poor, should receive an education according to their capacity. The subsequent appropriation of the revenues of the medieval Church by the Crown and the laity deprived the Reformed Church of the resources needed to carry out this scheme, but the idea behind it was never lost sight of, and in 1696 the Scottish Parliament enacted that it should be the duty of the heritors (landowners) of every parish to provide 'a commodious house for a school' and the salary of a teacher.[2]

'It was,' says Ernest Barker, 'on the basis of these national schools, and the national universities to which they led, that Scottish thought flourished so vigorously in the eighteenth century, and that Scotland was able to become the teacher in moral and metaphysical philosophy not only of England, but also of France and Germany. . . . In this way the Scottish nation found itself, not only as a Church, but also, through the influence of the Church, as an educational society, united in a common devotion to knowledge and pure thought.'[3] The enthusiasm for education shown by the pioneers of this Presbyterian régime was, no doubt, largely due to their desire to propagate their religious doctrine, and it must also be said that they were often intolerant and even capable of persecution. They were, too, narrow in their social morality and rigorous in applying their discipline, but time

---

1. Ernest Barker, *National Character*, Methuen, 1927, p. 189.
2. *Public Education in Scotland*, H.M.S.O., for Scottish Education Department, 1955, p. 5.
3. *National Character*, p. 192.

softened these asperities and broadened their outlook. 'In all countries alike,' Tawney observes, 'in Holland, in America, in Scotland, in Geneva itself, the social theory of Calvinism went through the same process of development. It had begun by being the very soul of regimentation. It ended by being the vehicle of an almost utilitarian individualism.'[1]

There could be no better illustration of this changed attitude than the religious concordat embodied in the Education (Scotland) Act of 1918, referred to in Chapter 1. For under that statute most generous provision is made in this predominantly Presbyterian country for the kind of education desired by the Roman Catholics and Episcopalians. But, while the old asperities have vanished, there still survive from earlier times several social traditions, handed down through the Kirk, that provide an excellent background for educational growth – orderly home life, a strong sense of responsibility, a respect for intellectual vigour, and a healthy ambition to be 'a lad (or lass) of pairts'.

THE ENGLISH REVOLUTION

In England the Reformation followed a very different course from that which it took in Scotland. In Scotland the General Assembly of the Churches became all important, and after the Act of Union (1707) was the only body representative of the nation. In England, on the other hand, 'the Reformation impulses were controlled and directed by the state at every point'.[2] Elizabeth with her political acumen, assisted by William Cecil's shrewd counsel, strove valiantly to accomplish a reasonable settlement of Church and State relationship – a *via media* – that would harmonize with the nationalism characteristic of that period.

The internal organization of the Church was left in its medieval form with a hierarchy of state-appointed bishops; doctrinally a good deal of scope was left for varying shades of belief, Catholic, Lutheran, Calvinist. It was a typical English compromise settlement, and through all the changes of centuries it has lasted ever since.[3]

1. *Religion and the Rise of Capitalism*, p. 205.
2. A. L. Rowse, *The Spirit of English History*, Cape, 1943, p. 48.
3. ibid., p. 53.

Although the Church continued to be administered much as it had been in pre-Reformation days, it became, as Tawney observes, 'the ecclesiastical department of the state, and religion was used to lend a moral sanction to secular social policy'.[1] Queen Elizabeth, said Carlyle, 'tuned her pulpits' as governing persons now strive to tune their morning newspapers.[2] Education continued to be regarded as part of the Church's province, and teachers were required to conform and were, no doubt, regarded by those in authority as valuable dispensers of propaganda. From Elizabeth's day onwards attempts were made, says F. W. Maitland, 'to force people to accept the doctrine and worship of the Church as defined by statute'.[3] Teachers were often special targets of such enforcing legislation. For example, schoolmasters and all persons who had taken a university degree were among those required under the Act of Supremacy (1562) to take the oath of allegiance, declaring the Queen to be the only supreme governor 'as well in all spiritual or ecclesiastical causes as temporal'. And under the Recusancy Act of 1580 a schoolmaster who taught without possessing a bishop's licence or who did not attend the parish church laid himself open to a year's imprisonment.

Such regimentation of teachers was not confined to religious or political issues. The zeal for uniformity led to interference with the curriculum and to authoritarian comments on methods of teaching grammar. All teachers of Latin – the mainstay of the grammar-school time-table – were required by Henry VIII to use Lily's Latin grammar because of 'the great hindrance which heretofore hath been through the diversity of grammars and teachings'. Similar injunctions were repeated by Edward VI, Mary, and Elizabeth, and in the latter's reign the requirement about the use of Lily's grammar was reinforced by the statement that 'there is but one bestnesse, not only in everything, but also in the manner of everything'.[4] This grammar book had a long run as an official favourite. For again in the Canons of the Church of

1. *Religion and the Rise of Capitalism*, p. 154.
2. Quoted by Christopher Hill in *The English Revolution, 1640*, Lawrence and Wishart, 1940, p. 15.
3. *The Constitutional History of England*, Cambridge University Press, 1908, p. 514.
4. See Adamson, op. cit., pp. 124–5.

England of 1604 schoolmasters are required to use this particular book and brusquely told they must use 'none other'.

Elizabeth and her advisers had, however, too much political wisdom to make the mistake of alienating the teaching profession; and teachers enjoyed under her authoritarian régime certain benefits such as relief from taxation and exemption from services required of other citizens. It is interesting to note that Elizabeth herself made little use of this prescribed grammar. Her tutor, Roger Ascham, when advocating double translation as a method of learning languages, tells of her remarkable prowess as a translator although 'she never took Greek nor Latin grammar in her hand after the first declining of a noun and verb'. And with commendable pride in the scholarship of his illustrious pupil, he contends that 'there be few now in both universities or elsewhere in England that be in both tongues comparable with Her Majesty'.[1]

When James I (1603–25) followed Elizabeth on the throne the country was at peace at home and abroad. England had become a nation-state, increasingly prosperous. Although James I's reign, while generally peaceful, was in many ways an eventful one, no important changes took place. 'In society, in economics, in the religious convictions of the people,' says Trevelyan, 'it is difficult to name any great difference between the England of Shakespeare and the England of Pym.'[2] With hindsight we can regard the history of these twenty or so years as the calm before the great storm. For under the surface profound changes in the structure of society and the distribution of wealth were maturing, which, combined with religious and personal issues, were to culminate in revolution and civil war.

It was revolution on a big scale, comparable with the French Revolution of 1789 and the revolution launched in Russia in 1917.[3] Often called the Puritan Revolution, it was essentially a war of religion with Anglicans fighting on one side and Presbyterians on the other. It was, however, no less a political struggle:

1. Quoted by R. H. Quick, *Essays on Educational Reformers*, Longmans, 1898 ed. p. 88.
2. *England under the Stuarts*, Methuen, 1912 ed., p. 3.
3. A. L. Rowse, *The Spirit of English History*, p. 61.

Parliament *v.* the King with several important civil liberties at stake. There were, too, important economic factors: new wealth was creating a new gentry, merchants and traders. This upward social mobility, this new distribution of wealth was changing the balance of society and creating 'the fundamental social force from which the seventeenth-century Revolution sprang'.[1]

It was above all else a struggle for power, and one in which education figured prominently. Education was particularly involved in the religious aspect of the conflict, for both the Anglicans and their Presbyterian adversaries used it in turn to propagate their respective interpretation of Christianity. There was trouble as soon as James I ascended the throne – the episodes known as the Millenary Petition and the Hampton Court Conference. This was an attempt by a number of Puritan clergy, who were not separatists, to get some rather minor grievances redressed. They obtained little for their pains, and, as president of the Conference, the King treated them brusquely, making no attempt at reconciliation.

Shortly afterwards the Convocation of Canterbury met and adopted the famous Canons of 1604, making it still more difficult for a good Puritan to accept the Ordinances of the Church. Many clergy were, in effect, driven out of the Church, and became the spiritual leaders of the growing opposition to the Establishment. Of the Canons, two (nos. 77 and 79) deal at length with the duties of schoolmasters. What they promulgate is very much the mixture previously prescribed by Edward VI and Elizabeth – the bishop's licence, attendance at Church, recognition of the authority of the Crown in matters ecclesiastical as well as civil, and acknowledgement of the orthodoxy of the Church of England. Nor in its authoritarian zeal for uniformity did Convocation forget Lily's Latin grammar. The said schoolmasters were enjoined to 'expound and teach no other grammar than that published by authority of Henry VIII and successively continued in the times of Edward VI and Queen Elizabeth of most happy memory'.

This despotic control of education reached a peak when James I's son, Charles I, having dissolved Parliament, began in 1629 that

1. ibid., p. 64. See also Christopher Hill's essay in *The English Revolution, 1640*, Lawrence and Wishart, 1940.

calamitous period of personal rule that culminated in the Revolution. The King's two principal advisers during this final phase were Strafford and Archbishop Laud. Both were men of high quality but with a totalitarian zest for regimentation and both, like their King, died on the scaffold. Education was one of Laud's responsibilities, and as he had been a successful president of an Oxford college and a forceful vice-chancellor it might be thought that he had a particularly useful background for this task. Laud apparently thought so himself. For at Oxford he had battled triumphantly with Puritan dons, and came to high office convinced that by a vigorous enforcement of law and order he could win another victory over Puritanism at the national level. 'England was to him,' says Trevelyan, 'another Oxford, a place whence Puritanism, at first blustering and assertive, could soon be driven out by methodical application of college discipline.'[1]

Laud used education ruthlessly in his campaign to enforce uniformity in religion. 'He was,' wrote an eminent Nonconformist of our time, 'a devout man to whom his religion was the greatest of realities, and he had the kind of ruthless sincerity that comes very near to fanaticism.'[2] He stretched to the full the wide powers of the Court of High Commission, of which he was president – this court was established by the Act of Supremacy in Elizabeth's reign to deal with jurisdiction of an ecclesiastical character – and under his pressure the bishops applied to schools their considerable disciplinary powers and, especially, those designed to ensure that all teachers were loyal and orthodox members of the Church of England. Laud's foolish attempt to force his prayer-book on Scotland hastened the day of revolution. Imprisoned in the Tower in 1641 by the revolutionary Long Parliament, he was executed four years later. He was then seventy-two years old, and it is not surprising that the memory of this brutal deed long survived in Anglican households to inflame smouldering animosities.

EDUCATION IN A REVOLUTIONARY SETTING

The Presbyterians in power were as keen about uniformity as the

1. *England under the Stuarts*, p. 167.
2. W. B. Selbie, *Nonconformity*, Thornton Butterworth: H.U.L., 1912, p. 63.

Anglicans, and just as ready to apply compulsion. And, like the Anglicans, they believed that within the nation there should be only one Church and that all citizens should conform to its beliefs and forms of worship. If, says Tawney, Puritanism 'broke the discipline of the Church of Laud and the State of Strafford, it did so but as a step towards erecting a more rigorous discipline of its own'. And he adds, 'A godly discipline was, indeed, the very ark of the Puritan covenant.'[1] As the Presbyterians and their sympathizers dominated the Long Parliament, they were able to shape policy and, seeking to win support for their views by means of education, they beat 'the drum ecclesiastic' pretty vigorously in schools and in the two universities. As Milton observed, the 'new Presbyter' was but 'old Priest writ large'.[2]

Events in Wales provide, perhaps, the clearest illustration of the aims and methods of the Presbyterians. Although two of the signatories of Charles I's death warrant were Welshmen, the principality as a whole was intensely royalist. From a Presbyterian standpoint, therefore, it was a black spot in sore need of conversion. So in 1650 Parliament passed an Act for the better Propagation and Preaching of the Gospel in Wales. Commissioners were appointed to administer the Act and they ejected, for various reasons, about 300 clergy from their benefices. 'Approvers' were then designated to find suitable 'godly and painful men' to replace them. The Act also provided for a system of schools in Wales, and the 'Approvers' were entrusted with the important duty of selecting as staff schoolmasters suitable 'for the teaching of children in piety and literature'. The 'Approvers' had a difficult task, for in the Wales of that day Puritans were in short supply. Sixty new schools were opened, but the policy had not time to prove its worth before it was cut short by the Restoration in 1660. That it met with a poor response can be gleaned from the fact that only twenty-one of these sixty schools managed to sur-

1. *Religion and the Rise of Capitalism*, p. 193
2. The word 'Puritan' was coined in Elizabeth I's reign, and applied derisively to those who wanted to 'purify' the ceremonial and liturgy of the Church of England of that period. It was later used, but no longer derisively, to denote Presbyterians and others with Calvinist leanings inside or outside the Church. And its meaning is now often extended (but not as a rule in America) to include the 'Separatists' of the seventeenth century, e.g. Congregationalists or Baptists. See the article on 'Puritanism' by Ernest Barker in his *Church, State, and Study*, Methuen, 1930.

vive to 1660.[1] It has been estimated that about that time Puritans did not constitute more than 5 per cent of the population of Wales. Very different was the situation a century later, when Wales was rapidly becoming a stronghold of Nonconformity.

The established Church of England and Wales was, from a strictly legal standpoint, Presbyterian for fifteen years. The ordinances adopted by the Long Parliament for ensuring that schoolmasters were doctrinally suitable and not 'derogatory to the government now established' were drastic and detailed. Regional committees were set up in different parts of the country, charged with the duty of 'proceeding against all scandalous, malignant, and ill-affected clergymen, scholars, Fellows of colleges, and schoolmasters'. But in spite of all the ejecting and approving the Presbyterians' rule was nothing like so thorough in its pursuit of uniformity as that of the Anglicans under Archbishop Laud.

There was, for example, no case of ejection of a schoolmaster by the Commissioners for the Propagation of the Gospel in Wales, and it is interesting to note that the commissioners, possibly moved by sympathy for the ejected families, granted certificates to teach to eight clergymen who had been removed from their benefices, thus enabling them to teach in the new schools. There were, too, in England many examples of ejected clergymen or schoolmasters who established private schools, some meeting with considerable success. Several of the ejected clergy not only opened schools but also wrote to good purpose about education. Charles Hoole is an illustrious example: ejected from his Lincolnshire benefice he taught in private schools in London and wrote his well-known *A New Discovery of the Old Art of Teaching School*.[2]

One reason why the Presbyterian ordinances were not always rigorously enforced was that in many parts of the country this disciplinary system proved very unpopular. The dour austerity, the regimentation, and the denials of freedom were hotly resented; and what Trevelyan calls 'the prospect of intolerable dreariness' aroused hostility in many places. Against this background there

1. W. A. L. Vincent, *The State and School Education, 1640–1660*, p. 96.
2. See W. A. L. Vincent, ibid., pp. 66, 67.

was a weary struggle for supremacy between the Presbyterian zealots in Parliament and the Independents in the Army. With the triumph of the latter under the leadership of Cromwell, we reach an important milestone in the story of the government of education in this country. For the Independents brought into the centre of the political and religious arena the idea of toleration – 'the equal liberty of all' – which, after many grievous setbacks, eventually wrought a transformation in our conduct of educational affairs.

SOME ASPECTS OF THE REVOLUTION

By bringing the idea of free churches into the centre of the stage, the Independents and left-wing Puritans rendered education a great service. For thereby they sowed the seed of an alternative to the belief that there should be but one Church co-terminous with the nation.

They objected to that system in both its senses. They rejected the identification of Church and nation, and claimed that a Church might be, and properly ought to be, a 'gathered' body, voluntarily formed, which consisted of those members of the nation (and *only* of those members of the nation) who felt themselves called to join. They rejected equally the method of church government which vested the national king with the position of supreme governor, and they claimed that each 'gathered' body, just as it was freely and voluntarily formed, should also be freely and voluntarily governed as a free Church.[1]

These dissenting churches also created the conception of intimate democracy that later proved so valuable in the local administration of education and in the development of the various voluntary societies concerned with education. 'Their genuine experienced democracy,' observes A. D. Lindsay, 'was not political, but the democracy of a voluntary society – a society which did not use force in the putting into practice of its decisions, but was a fellowship of discussion. They assumed that each member contributed to the discussion what he had to say, and that then men came to some agreement, to what Quakers were to call "the sense of the meeting". . . . Thus the Puritans of the Left, from

1. Ernest Barker, *Britain and the British People*, Oxford University Press, 1942, pp. 84–5. See also Barker's *Cromwell*, Cambridge University Press, 1937, pp. 30–46.

their experience of the congregation, had an active experience of a satisfactory democratic life which rested on consent and on the resolution of differences by discussion.'[1] Today this intimate kind of democracy, that can be such an effective way of reaching an acceptable decision, is often superseded in local government by a less amicable procedure in which the prior conclusions of rival caucuses determine 'the sense of the meeting'.

There were other ideas of importance to the government of education that found expression during these revolutionary years. Some were political like the egalitarian views of the Levellers, for example, Colonel Rainborow's famous assertion, 'the poorest he that is in England hath a life to live as the greatest he'. There was a lively concern, too, about science and technology – views about study and research that resemble some of the belated aspirations of our own time. It was not a wholly one-sided interest. The Parliamentarians were, generally speaking, the main supporters of scientific advance but it certainly cannot be said that all Royalists were indifferent to it. Much of the innovating impetus was due to Bacon's continuing influence, and he was in politics no friend of the Puritans, although he deprecated their persecution. It should be noted, too, that the Royal Society founded in 1662 not only had the backing of Charles II, but also included among its founder members men of various political sympathies. It could be argued that a revolutionary atmosphere often creates an urge for technological advance: for there is evidence to support this contention in the England of 1640, France of 1789, Russia of 1917, and in the world revolution in process today.

It was, however, from the Parliament side that most of the demand for scientific education came in this country in the mid seventeenth century. No one had more influence on educational thought under the Commonwealth than did the famous Czech educationist, Comenius. He derived much of his inspiration from the writings of Francis Bacon, and shared to the full the latter's enthusiasm for scientific study and research.[2] Among educational

1. *The Modern Democratic State*, Oxford University Press, 1943, Vol. I, pp. 117–18.

2. See an interesting chapter on 'Bacon and Comenius' in Adamson's *Pioneers of Modern Education*, Cambridge University Press, 1905.

reformers of this period the advocacy of science was often combined with a contempt for the scholasticism of the universities and the narrow classical curriculum of the grammar schools. But some were able to combine a zeal for modern studies with an appreciation of the learning of antiquity. John Wilkins is an example of a leading scholar of those revolutionary times who had a regard for both cultures, the ancient as well as that of the moderns; and his career is also interesting as an illustration of the vicissitudes of academic life in a revolutionary age.

The son of an Oxford goldsmith, he was an ardent Baconian and a leading member of the small influential group whose meetings culminated after the Restoration in the founding of the Royal Society. In 1648 Parliament set up a commission to reform Oxford University, a Royalist stronghold; and, as a good supporter of the Parliamentary cause, Wilkins was made Warden of Wadham, a college founded earlier in the century on the site of an old friary that like other monasteries had suffered the fate of dissolution. The good Warden married Oliver Cromwell's sister, and later made a name for himself by publishing his *Mathematical Magic*. In this book he pays a high tribute to 'the mechanical discoveries' of the Romans, and suggests that the modern world cannot hope to surpass them. 'It was,' says Sir George Clark after noting Wilkins' veneration for the achievements of antiquity, 'a learned book, but it was not the work of a man who looked only backwards. It has speculations about submarines, and flying, and perpetual motion.'[1] Wilkins was prominent as an advocate for funds for the promotion of scientific and technical education, and frequently deplored the inadequacy of the money available. Such parsimony, he observed, 'robs the world of many excellent inventions'. He contrasted the niggardly response to his appeals with the generosity of Alexander the Great, who paid for the collections of materials for Aristotle's scientific studies; and Wilkins made a comment on this point that deserves to be better known: 'The reason why the world hath not many Aristotles,' he said, 'is because it hath so few Alexanders.'[2] The Restoration

1. G. N. Clark, *Science and Social Welfare in the Age of Newton*, Oxford University Press, 2nd ed., 1949, p. 9.
2. ibid., p. 12.

did not halt his career, and six years after Charles I I became king, this enterprising brother-in-law of the great Protector was enthroned as Bishop of Chester. He and his successor in that see were both Fellows of the Royal Society, but no occupant of the see has since been similarly honoured.

The universities were deeply involved in the struggle for power. For four years Oxford was the Royalist H.Q.: it 'ceased to be a place of learning and was converted into a camp'.[1] Cambridge, too, had Royalist sympathies and, says Macaulay, 'condemned in severe terms the violence and treachery of the turbulent men who had maliciously endeavoured to turn the stream of succession out of the ancient channel'. It is not surprising, therefore, that when the Parliamentarians gained power they sought to rid the universities of hostile influences. In 1659 Parliament resolved: 'That the Universities and Schools of Learning shall be so countenanced and reformed, as that they may become Nurseries of Piety and Learning.' In both universities there were many ejections: in Cambridge twelve Heads of Colleges and 181 Fellows were removed.[2] But the 'turbulent men' were by no means enemies of the universities: 'rather they sought to awaken them from supineness and lethargy, and to encourage discipline and sound learning'.[3]

Cromwell, when receiving an honorary D.C.L. at Oxford, assured the university that he and his supporters knew no Commonwealth could flourish without learning: and that so far from depleting the resources of the universities 'they purposed to add more'. And so, indeed, they did, providing under the Commonwealth Acts of 1649 a specific grant of £20,000 a year for the increase of the maintenance of the masterships of the colleges of both universities.[4] They did not tinker with the constitutions of the universities and their colleges; and, in spite of the many new faces in the senior common rooms, changes were relatively few. 'The University,' writes Marriott about Oxford during the Revolutionary period, 'was indeed "visited" by one commission

1. J. A R. Marriott, *Oxford in National History*, Clarendon Press, 1933, p. 115.
2. See Adamson, *Pioneers of Modern Education*, p. 119.
3. W. A. L. Vincent, op. cit., p. 88.
4. J. E. G. Montmorency, *State Intervention in English Education*, Cambridge University Press, 1902, p. 87.

after another, but exhibited its customary ingenuity in devising methods of "passive resistance"'; consequently the disturbance of academical continuity 'was less than might have been expected'.[1]

For such progress as was achieved during these unsettled times, some credit should be given to the quality of the men who replaced the ejected Masters and Fellows. From the standpoint of university administration the most notable was Cromwell's famous chaplain, John Owen, who became Dean of Christ Church and Oxford's Vice-Chancellor. 'Tolerant alike by nature and profession,' says Marriott of this wise Independent, '. . . Owen practically ruled the University for the best part of a decade (1651–9) and, on the whole, with eminent success.'[2] The interest shown by Cromwell and his supporters in university education was not confined to Oxford and Cambridge. During their régime the universities of Glasgow, Edinburgh, and Aberdeen all benefited financially: and in 1657 letters patent were issued by Cromwell for the establishment of a university at Durham in houses formerly occupied by the Dean and Chapter. This project, however, did not mature, and at the Restoration the Dean and his Anglican colleagues resumed possession of their houses, and Durham had to wait for its university until it was given a Royal Charter in 1832.[3]

The educational reformers of this Revolutionary period also championed the idea of compulsory education for all under the auspices of the state. 'All Youth of both sexes should be put to school' is the title of one of the chapters in Comenius's *Great Didactic*; and he urged that the state should establish a system of primary schools, at which attendance should be universal and compulsory. He also advocated the provision of a secondary stage for pupils of suitable intellectual calibre. And Harrington in his *Oceana*, contemplating society from the standpoint of a political philosopher, is almost more emphatic about the need for a democratic system of education as a foundation of the Common-

1. *Oxford in National History*, p. 138.

2. ibid., p. 138.

3. Adamson, *Pioneers in Modern Education*, p. 105. See also article by Joan Simon on 'Educational Policies and Programmes during the English Revolution' in *Modern Quarterly*, Spring 1949.

wealth. He is a most interesting character – a devoted admirer and friend of Charles I and yet a convinced republican. 'No political writer,' says Dr G. P. Gooch, 'has discerned with greater clearness the importance of education in the life and well-being of a State. A better system of instruction had been one of the petitions of Milton to the Protector in *Defensio Secunda*, and a scheme had been outlined in the *Letter to Hartlib*; but Harrington came forward with practical proposals, anticipating in a very striking way the modern system of universal and compulsory education under the control of the State.'[1]

Harrington advocated compulsion because in his view parents could not always be trusted to consider their children's interests. The state, he maintained, should provide schools for all, and the age of compulsory attendance should be from nine to fifteen. Parents should pay fees if they could afford them, but, if not able to pay, their children should be accepted 'gratis'. The magistrates should 'animadvert and punish' parents who neglected to send their children to school if they were between the specified ages.

To the Commonwealth reformers we owe yet another idea of great significance in modern education – namely that of a new type of secondary school, as an alternative to the grammar school. 'Realism' was a keynote of their educational thought, and its meaning can be summed up in the phrase 'things not words'. Bacon set the idea on its course, and Comenius made it a basic feature of his educational planning. This new teaching is a constant theme of educationists of this period: for example, in John Dury's *Reformed School*, which has a preface by Hartlib, that influential Polish exile with a liking for schemes and a passionate yearning for educational advance. There are echoes of 'realism' in Milton's *Tractate* and it is prominent in the writings of the economist, Sir William Petty, who stresses the value to this nation of such studies as 'Mathematicks, Mechanicks and Physick' and also advocates the provision of a 'College of Tradesmen for the Advancement of all Mechanical Arts and Manufactures'. This concept of 'real education' has had a chequered history in this

1. *Political Thought in England from Bacon to Halifax*, Oxford University Press (Home University Library), 1914, p. 117.

country: it has at different times, and often without much encouragement, found expression in dissenting academies, and in higher grade, central, and junior technical schools. At long last it seems to be coming into its own in the secondary modern, technical, and comprehensive schools that have developed since 1944.

During this momentous seventeenth century, the western tradition of education, especially its English version, was being exported to North America. Features, both good and bad, of the English heritage were transplanted: and all the principal contestants in the religious warfare were making their respective contributions to educational planning in the New World – Anglicans in Virginia, Catholics in Maryland, Quakers in Pennsylvania, and Puritans in New England. New England has a very special niche in the history of education, and the Massachusetts Act of 1647 requiring a general provision of schools including grammar schools, where numbers justified it, is a remarkable piece of forward-looking legislation. There is some doubt about the extent of schooling provided under this Act, but there is no doubt that in New England education was from the first a high priority, and it has been estimated that within two generations some twenty-seven grammar schools were founded.

It is probable that, as with the Puritans in England, the propagation of the approved form of Christianity was in these early American communities a principal motive for the establishment of schools, but it was by no means the only consideration. Many of the Puritan leaders, including of course the ministers of religion, were themselves well educated and among them were men and women who valued education as a basis of society and a source of individual well-being. There were also economic motives. Some of the leading Puritans belonged, like their counterparts in England, to the rising middle class; and wanted a good education for their own families and also the kind of schooling that would provide the new communities with good tradesmen and reliable artisans. The need for university education was recognized at an early stage: for, as well as a respect for learning, there was the realization that without such education the churches could not have the benefit of an educated ministry. Harvard was founded in 1636, and Yale in 1701.

The Puritan colonies had different ideas about the relationship of church and state. Rhode Island, for example, under the influence of Roger Williams allowed complete freedom of conscience, and so did Pennsylvania. Massachusetts, on the other hand, was a rigid and oligarchic church-state, in which all who deviated in doctrine or conduct were severely disciplined or expelled. It had no use for tolerance as these bitter words of Thomas Dudley, a founder and Deputy Governor, show:

> Let men of God in courts and churches watch
> O'er such as do a toleration hatch,
> Lest that ill egg bring forth a cockatrice
> To poison all with heresy and vice.[1]

THE NECESSITY OF TOLERANCE

The Commonwealth reformers had pointed the way to educational advance, and it is reasonable to believe that, if their ideas had been generally accepted, a national system of education on modern lines would soon have begun to develop in this country. But progress of that kind is impossible without tolerance and it took us over 200 more years to acquire just enough of that precious attribute to make educational legislation on a national scale practicable. The dreams of the educational reformers quickly evaporated with the passing of the Commonwealth; Milton retired to write that 'great epic of defeat', *Paradise Lost*, and poor Hartlib spent his days composing begging letters in order to rescue his family from destitution.

With the Restoration of the Stuarts power passed to men who supported the church and regarded dissenters as misguided and subversive. So they launched a policy of suppression enacting, as their main instrument, the vindictive Clarendon Code with its four penal laws: the Corporation Act, which excluded dissenters from public life; the Conventicle Act, which prevented them from worshipping together; the Five Mile Act, which barred their ministers from living in centres of population; and the Act of Uniformity which stopped them from functioning as ministers

1. Quoted by Deane Jones, *The English Revolution, 1603–1714*, Heinemann, 1931, p. 273.

of religion and 'instructing or teaching youth in any private house or family as schoolmaster'.

It was not only a quarrel about religion: it was also largely a political battle with social undertones. 'The object of the Clarendon Code,' says Trevelyan, 'was to prevent the revival of the Roundhead party, and to avenge the wrongs suffered by Anglicans and Cavaliers. But the spirit of the persecution was not ecclesiastical; it was not a heresy hunt.'[1] This renewal of strife had important consequences for education. It intensified the cleavage in the nation, and before the turbulent century closed, two distinct parties were sparring with each other in the political arena – the Tories, who were normally loyal Churchmen and whole-hearted supporters of the Anglican attitude to education, and the Whigs who, like their Roundhead fathers, were staunch champions of dissent. As a main battleground education suffered severely, and in unhealthy rivalry Anglicanism and Dissent developed different educational traditions. So bitter and persistent was the sectarian strife that not until 1870 was it possible to embark on a national system: and then legislation was only possible by the adoption of a dual scheme based on a most ingenious compromise.

Just as the martyrdom of Christians under the Roman Empire encouraged the growth of Christianity, so persecution under the Clarendon Code generated nonconformity. By penalizing all who did not give 'unfeigned consent' to everything in the Anglican Prayer Book, the Act of Uniformity drove many more Puritans out of the church. Becoming 'nonconformists', often most reluctantly, they reinforced the dissenting minority – the Independents, the Baptists, the Separatists, the Quakers, and others. Indeed, it has been said, 'the Act of Uniformity of 1662 is by many taken as the real beginning of Nonconformity'.[2] While often mean and pettifogging, the persecution could also be very brutal: John Bunyan, it will be remembered, spent twelve years in Bedford gaol, and the saintly Richard Baxter was imprisoned by the notorious Judge Jeffreys after having been

---

1. *English Social History*, p. 256.
2. E. A. Payne, *The Free Church Tradition in the Life of England*, S.C.M. Press, 1944, p. 45.

described by him as 'an old rogue, a schismatical knave, a hypocritical villain'.

One surprising outcome of the Act of Uniformity was the establishment of a new type of educational institution, the Dissenting Academy. About twenty of these academies were founded between 1662 and 1668, and another thirty between 1690 and 1750. Their initial purpose was the training of ministers of religion since dissenters were barred from the universities, but because of the quality and scope of the education that they provided many nonconforming parents sent their sons to them at about the age of fifteen. Staffed by ejected ministers, dons, and schoolmasters, they offered a curriculum which, while giving prominence to divinity, Latin, and Greek, also, reflecting the realist influence of Comenius, included mathematics, science, and often geography.

The academies often led a precarious existence and, largely as a result of the Five Mile Act, some had to change their location to avoid prosecution. But they survived the assaults of their enemies, including a particularly vicious attack in Queen Anne's reign which led to the passing of the Schism Act of 1714 which forbade anyone not being a member of the Church of England to keep a school. Among the pupils of the academies were a few who became famous, e.g. Daniel Defoe (Stoke Newington) and Joseph Priestley (Daventry). Some – one of life's little ironies – made their mark in the Church: for example, Secker, who became Archbishop of Canterbury, and Bishop Butler, renowned for his *Analogy of Religion*. Two – yet another touch of irony – became leading Tory statesmen, Harley and St John, and they showed their ingratitude by helping to promote the iniquitous Schism Act. Happily that Act was repealed five years later but, although the academies subsequently prospered for a while, they did not survive for long. Various factors contributed to bring about their decline and fall towards the end of the eighteenth century. Undoubtedly a principal cause of their eclipse was that there was much less persecution; without the stimulus of martyrdom the academies found it difficult to maintain their early enthusiasm. Another reason for their decline was the growth of private academies that concentrated on the more utilitarian aspects of the academy curriculum and so appealed to middle-class parents – mainstays of nonconformity – who wanted their boys to do well in business. But the most disruptive factor in the life of the Dissenting Academies was internal strife, perhaps the deadliest of all the diseases to which educational (and other) institutions are liable. For during the second half of the eighteenth century many tutors in the academies were influenced by the spirit of rationalism then gaining ground, and these 'rational dissenters' – Priestley was an outstanding one – were often at loggerheads with their more orthodox colleagues.

The latter tried to stem the rationalist tide and safeguard traditional doctrine, and with this object students in many academies were required on admission to subscribe to a definite creed. This rigidity alienated some of the abler supporters of the academies and so hastened their dissolution.[1] But their influence continued. Some developed as colleges for the education of ministers, but even more important was the fact that their realist bias was adopted and passed on to higher grade and central schools by the better private academies. 'These commercial academies and private schools,' says the Spens Report, 'undoubtedly had many faults, but they were more receptive of new ideas and more ready to experiment than the old endowed Grammar Schools, and subsequent reforms in the curriculum can be largely traced to their influence.'[2]

Although nonconformists suffered grievously their pains and penalties were not so severe nor so prolonged as those endured by Roman Catholics.[3] Under laws passed in Elizabeth's reign every Catholic was compelled to attend Anglican services, the celebration of the Mass was suppressed, and the Catholic priesthood proscribed. With priests and university dons in exile, Catholic education was brought to a standstill except under clandestine arrangements and at great risk. Magistrates were

1. See Irene Parker, *Dissenting Academies in England,* Cambridge University Press, 1914, p. 136.

2. *Report of the Consultative Committee on Secondary Education,* H.M.S.O., 1938, p. 13.

3. For a scholarly account of English Roman Catholic education from the Reformation to the fall of James II, see A. C. F. Beales, *Education under Penalty,* Athlone Press, 1963.

not always zealous in executing these harsh laws, and consequently there was some variation in their administration. But, says Lecky,

had such laws been rigorously enforced they must have led to a general Catholic emigration or have dyed every scaffold with Popish blood; and as it was, many Catholics perished in England to whom it is the merest sophistry to deny the title of martyrs for their faith. The conspiracy of Guy Faux to blow up the Parliament, the fable of the Popish plot which led to the effusion of torrents of innocent blood, and, perhaps still more, the baseless calumny which attributed the Fire of London to the Priests, sustained the anti-Catholic fanaticism.[1]

But eventually the tide turned and, surprisingly, it was the French Revolution that particularly helped to establish Roman Catholic education in this country. For as a result of the Revolution the English colleges in France and Belgium had to close down, and their teachers sought refuge here. They were made welcome, and instead of hostility there was now hospitality. The English Catholics, it has been well said,

became refugees for a second time, but now they fled towards their native shores. Prejudice against Catholics in England was gradually disappearing. Although the disabling Acts were not entirely abolished, some measure of relief was passed by the Government in 1778. . . . In these circumstances the English Colleges were repatriated without hindrance. Douai College moved to Ushaw, and the Jesuits of St Omer to Stonyhurst. The Benedictine College of St Gregory gave rise to Downside School, and that of Dieuleward continued its existence at Ampleforth. The Cis-alpine scholars from exiled colleges founded their own college at Oscott in 1794. Thus at the end of the century the Catholics in England possessed half a dozen colleges with an established tradition which could rival the great public schools of the Anglicans.[2]

THE ESTABLISHED CHURCH AND ITS RIVALS

Mistrust was so deep-rooted that it was difficult for toleration to gain a foothold. But the time came when people were utterly weary of religious strife. 'At last,' says Trevelyan, describing the situation after the proclamation of William and Mary in 1689,

1. *History of England in the Eighteenth Century*, Vol. I, 2nd ed., Longmans, 1879, p. 272.
2. N. Hans, *Comparative Education*, Routledge and Kegan Paul, 1949, p. 116.

'the time had come when English Protestants were ready to let one another worship God . . . Like dogs that have been flogged off each other, Anglican and Puritan lay down and snarled.'[1] In the Toleration Act of the same year came the first modest concession to nonconformists: those who had taken the oaths of allegiance and supremacy were allowed to absent themselves from Church without penalty provided they were neither Papists nor Unitarians. But there was a growing humanity in the administration of the law and this, as Macaulay observes, should remind us that much depends on the spirit in which laws are administered.

The letter of the law, however, continued to be harsh and Blackstone, the great legal commentator, writing in the middle of the eighteenth century, still speaks of 'the crime of nonconformity'.[2] The removal of oppressive statutes came much later, and two great dates in the struggle for religious liberty are 1828, when the Test and Corporation Acts were repealed: and 1829, the year of the Catholic Emancipation Act.

Nonconformity was powerfully reinforced by the religious revivals that were such a notable feature of the eighteenth century. The first stirrings were felt in Wales where outstanding leaders, like Griffith Jones of Llanddowror, brought about a remarkable religious and educational awakening. He has been called 'the first of the field preachers', but he had also, like Wesley, great organizing ability as the success of his 'Circulating Schools' shows – over 150,000 pupils were taught in them during his lifetime. John Wesley and Whitefield inspired the great Methodist revival. 'No single figure,' said Birrell of John Wesley, 'inflamed so many minds, no single voice touched so many hearts. No other man did such a life's work for England.'[3] He, too, gave education a high priority. Of the school that he founded at Kingswood, he wrote 'I have spent more money, time, and care on this than on almost any design I ever had.'

Mindful of its founder's concern for education, Methodism has always attached importance to the provision of education of

1. *England under the Stuarts*, p. 449.
2. See Maitland, *The Constitutional History of England*, p. 516.
3. See Essay on 'John Wesley' in Augustine Birrell, *Miscellanies*, Elliot Stock, 1901.

high quality: its colleges of education, its schools, and its National Children's Home all have a fine tradition. From these great religious movements nonconformity acquired new strength both as regards quality and numbers. 'On the evidence,' says Halévy, estimating the relative strength of Anglicanism and noncomformity in 1815, 'we may conclude that while the nominal members of the Establishment still constituted an enormous majority, the Nonconformists already equalled, if they did not exceed, the Anglicans who practised their religion.'[1]

At the beginning of the nineteenth century education was confronting the Established Church with some difficult problems. Nominally it was still in control of education, but the task of providing it was becoming more and more formidable, and it was only one part of its spiritual responsibilities.

Under the stress of the great economic changes, the whole aspect of England was altering, the population had increased from 5,500,000 in 1750 to 9,000,000 in 1800 and large new areas, filled with teeming humanity, were left without pastoral charge or guidance.[2]

Anglicans had played a big part in the charity school movement in all its aspects – charity schools, ragged schools, Sunday schools – and had done valuable pioneer work in the organization of voluntary service. 'To philanthropy in general,' says Miss Margaret Jones, discussing the administrative features of the charity school movement, 'it contributed, in a highly developed form, the idea of association as the machinery for philanthropic effort. Voluntary societies for all sorts and conditions of social work followed in the wake of the London S.P.C.K. and its sister societies.'[3]

However much as one may admire these philanthropic enterprises, they were ludicrously inadequate as a method of providing elementary education during a period when population was growing and industry expanding rapidly. There was, indeed, a desperate need for better educational provision: and in 1807 Samuel Whitbread introduced a Bill designed to secure a national

---

1. *A History of the English People in 1815*, Penguin Books, 1938, Vol. III, p. 51.
2. Spencer Leeson, *Christian Education*, p. 64.
3. *The Charity School Movement*, Cambridge Univerity Press, 1938, p. 346; a scholarly and most informative account of philanthropy in the eighteenth century.

system of rate-aided elementary education. Alas! it was rejected by the House of Lords largely upon the advice of the Archbishop of Canterbury, who objected to any system that put the control of education elsewhere than in the hands of the bishop of the diocese.[1] This but intensified the feeling so well described by Spencer Leeson as 'that angry resentment against the Anglican monopoly of the schools'.[2] In the following year Anglicans were confronted with a definite encroachment into what they were still inclined to regard exclusively as their territory: the Royal Lancastrian Society (later to become the British and Foreign School Society) was founded to promote elementary education of a non-sectarian character. To counter this move the Church founded The National Society for Promoting the Education of the Poor in the Principles of the Established Church. How these two societies competed with each other in acrimonious rivalry is a tale so often told that it need not be repeated here.

In 1833 the state began to help these societies in their impossible task by making small grants in respect of particular schools. These grants were paid through the medium of the societies, and this practice led in time to the creation of bodies representative of other religious interests. First came the Wesleyan Educational Committee, formed in the first year of Victoria's reign. The Congregational Board of Education followed six years later. In 1847 the Catholic Poor School Committee was founded, taking the place of an earlier organization known as the Catholic Institute. The Jews established several schools in the large towns, and they had a special committee for contacts with the State Education Department.

The Established Church had, therefore, certainly lost its monopoly but its educational provision far exceeded that of its rivals. Of the 8,798 assisted voluntary schools in 1870, 6,724 belonged to the Church of England, 1,691 were provided by the 'British and Foreign', and 383 owed allegiance to other religious bodies and interests. But the total provision was hopelessly insufficient. Only half the parishes in England and Wales had grant-earning schools: and in four rapidly growing industrial

1. J. L. and B. Hammond, *The Town Labourer*, Longmans, 1917, p. 57.
2. *Christian Education*, p. 62.

centres – Birmingham, Leeds, Liverpool, and Manchester – there was approved schooling for only about fifty per cent of the children of school age.

By the middle of the nineteenth century it was generally recognized in circles that shape policy that educational reform on a wide scale was long overdue. Commissions were appointed to inquire into different aspects. One Commission reported on the universities, and its report led to two reforming measures – the Oxford University Act of 1854 and a similar Act for Cambridge in 1856. These were followed in 1871 by the University Tests Act, which made nearly all academic posts open, regardless of creed, at Oxford and Cambridge, and also in the university that had been founded at Durham in 1832. The Clarendon Commission reported on public schools, and its conclusions led to the Public Schools Act of 1868. Similarly the Taunton Commission surveyed the problem of the endowed secondary schools, and this led to the Endowed Schools Act of 1869. The immensely difficult task of advising about the future of elementary education was entrusted to the Newcastle Commission which was asked to recommend 'measures for the extension of sound and cheap elementary instruction to all classes'. It began its deliberations in 1858 when the country was still counting the cost of the Crimean War (1854–6). That is the only excuse that can be made for the miserly emphasis on cheapness in the terms of reference: for England had never been so prosperous.

It reported in 1861, and among its conclusions were two that had an important bearing on future policy. One was a recommendation that the payment of grants to schools should be based on the results of a 'searching examination' of 'every child in every school' in such a way as 'to make the prospects and position of the teacher dependent to a considerable extent on the results of this examination'. This led to the introduction of the notorious system of 'payment by results' associated with the name of Robert Lowe, the Minister responsible for initiating it. The other conclusion of the Commissioners that profoundly affected future policy was that in their view it was most desirable that the state should continue to look to the religious societies for the motive power in providing elementary education. The state, they urged, should maintain the existing practice of assisting these societies with grants-in-aid. This greatly strengthened the case for voluntary schools when in 1870 Parliament at long last laid the foundations of a national system in the Elementary Education Act of that year. The religious compromise then hammered out, is still an essential cornerstone of our educational system. We must leave our consideration of it to the next chapter.

CHAPTER 4

Education and Politics

THE ENGLISH COMPROMISE

THE Victorians quarrelled interminably about religious education, but fortunately they were interested too in the arts of
democratic government and, not least, in the use of compromise as
a basis for legislation and progressive administration. Edmund
Burke had stressed its importance in a great speech during George
III's reign. 'All government,' he contended, 'indeed every human
benefit and enjoyment, every virtue, and every prudent act, is
founded on compromise and barter. We balance inconveniences;
we give and take; we remit some rights, that we may enjoy others;
and we choose rather to be happy citizens than subtle disputants.'[1]
Several of the leading Victorian publicists spoke and wrote about
the use of compromise, discussing its value in politics and its
ethics – for example, when acceptance of a compromise at
variance with your principles is justifiable.

Lecky, who cites the Elementary Education Act of 1870 to
illustrate his argument, maintains that 'there must be, both in the
Cabinet and in Parliament, perpetual compromise'. He regarded
'legitimate time-serving' as an important feature of a statesman's
outfit, and he insisted that whatever principles are at stake 'under
free governments, political questions and measures must be
adjusted to the wishes of the various sections of the people, and
this adjustment is a great work of statesmanship'.[2] John Morley
in his book *On Compromise* is more cautious and discusses the
demerits as well as the merits of compromise. He is critical of the
settlement embodied in the Elementary Education Act of 1870

1. *Speeches on America*, edited by A. D. Innes, Cambridge University Press, 1906,
p. 149.
2. *The Map of Life*, Longmans, 1913 ed., pp. 120, 141.

and uses it to illustrate his contention that 'the small reform may become the enemy of the great one'.[1] He apparently assumed – how mistaken he was – that voluntary schools were doomed: and it seemed to him wrong for the sake of agreement to give voluntary schools 'new comfort and strength' and so prolong their existence and postpone the advent of a truly national system in which voluntaryism had no part.

The Newcastle Commission presented its report about Elementary Education in 1861 and from then to 1870 innumerable pressure groups were at work urging various solutions of 'the religious question'. The conflicting opinions, canvassed with such acrimonious enthusiasm, make one wonder how any compromise could be devised that would win the approval of a parliamentary majority. The battle raged throughout the country and in the large towns there were meetings and counter meetings. Manchester constituted an Education Bill Committee to press for immediate legislation, and Birmingham established an Education League, which advocated the provision of free, unsectarian education, the cost to be borne by rates and taxes. Inspired by Joseph Chamberlain, then a young and fiery Radical, it carried out a nation-wide campaign, setting up about a hundred branch committees. As a counterblast the National Education Union was founded under Anglican auspices, its aim being 'to counteract the work of the Birmingham League and press for an increase of government grant, sufficient to enable the voluntary societies to meet the whole demand for elementary education'.

By 1870 the situation had become politically favourable for some measure of educational reform. The Liberals had just come back to office, thanks partly to the widening of the franchise by their Conservative opponents – Disraeli's famous 'leap in the dark'. The Liberals were in effect a new party, including the Whigs and a number of Radicals, many of whom owed their election to the votes of the newly-enfranchised working men. Gladstone, having recently succeeded Lord Palmerston as leader, was eager to press forward with reforms; and Disraeli, the leader of the Opposition, was no less keen on reform, having made his mark as the protagonist of Tory democracy. Thoughtful men in

1. *On Compromise*, Macmillan, 1877, p. 232.

both parties recognized that educational reform was overdue, and it is a reasonable assumption that if the Conservatives had been in office, they would have been just as ready as the Liberals to produce an Education Bill.

Traditionally the Conservatives were, as we noted in the last chapter, ardent supporters of Anglican causes, while the Liberals had inherited the Whig alliance with Dissent. But there were Anglicans among the Liberals – Gladstone was a devout Anglican – and there were non-Anglicans on the Conservative benches. In fact, a main characteristic of the prolonged debates on the 1870 Education Bill was the obliteration of normal party alignments – the party machine did not dominate in those days as it does now; in many of the discussions and divisions on this crucial measure Liberals and Conservatives fought as one in internecine strife against members of their own parties. Indeed, staunch Government supporters accused Gladstone of forcing the Bill through with the aid of Tory votes; and he rounded on them, not only admitting the charge but even glorying in it. 'Prejudice,' he thundered, 'has been attempted to be exerted against this Bill, because it has found considerable favour with the gentlemen opposite.' He chided them for thinking that there was something inherently wrong with a Government proposal that attracted Opposition support, and rebuked them for behaving as if members of the Opposition were their 'natural enemies'.

'Measures not men' runs the old adage once fiercely repudiated by Edmund Burke.[1] We certainly owe much to our three great Education Acts – those of 1870, 1902, and 1944 – but we are no less indebted to the men who shaped them and piloted them through Parliament. W. E. Forster who, as Vice-President of the Committee of Council on Education, was the Minister responsible for the 1870 Act was by temperament and experience singularly well fitted for the task of forging a compromise acceptable to a wide variety of religious and political interests. Of Quaker stock and schooling, he was deeply religious and had a strong social conscience with an abundance of human sympathy; but on his marriage to Dr Arnold's daughter, he had ceased to be a member of the Society of Friends without committing himself to

1. See *Thoughts on the Present Discontents* (near the end).

any other religious allegiance. His doctrinal detachment helped him in winning the support of various interests, and Anglicans and Dissenters alike appreciated his sincerity and integrity of mind. 'I am not a Dissenter,' he told the House of Commons, 'I wish that I could see my way clear to belong to any religious community.' Bradford was the centre of his business activity, the wool trade: and, burly and rough-hewn, he was the personification of those solid virtues which middle-class Victorians so greatly admired. There were many in all grades of society – Queen Victoria among them – who liked his unpolished ways and his forthright, blunt speech.

'On the whole, I think Forster has hit on the only plan that will work in so curious a country as England.'[1] So a distinguished London journalist, a Scot, wrote to his sister when Forster presented his Bill to the House of Commons. It was essentially Forster's Bill, his own ingenious masterpiece; but throughout the Parliamentary battle – some thirty sessions of critical and usually acrimonious debate – he had the support of Gladstone, 'now close on sixty years, approaching the climacteric and brief perfection of his political genius'.[2] Of the great Prime Minister's concern for university education there is ample evidence, but whether he was deeply interested in public education may be doubted: in his attitude to it he was very much the good squire of Hawarden, devoted to its parish church and its national schools. But his interventions in the debate were wise and adroit; and no doubt the fact that the Liberal Party, so closely associated with Dissent, was led by a great churchman helped many good Anglicans to discover virtues in the compromise that might otherwise have escaped their notice. Of his courage in backing the Bill there can be no question. For it was too favourable to voluntary schools to please his nonconformist supporters, and it was a principal cause of his party's defeat and Disraeli's return to power in 1874. 'Gladstone,' says Trevelyan approvingly, 'performed his various tasks as a national legislator without too nicely considering the electoral consequences.'[3]

1. W. R. Nicoll, *James McDonnell, Journalist,* Hodder and Stoughton, 1889, p. 349.
2. Trevelyan, *British History in the Nineteenth Century,* Longmans, 1922, p. 349.
3. ibid., p. 354.

After Parliament had accepted the compromise about religious education, as amended, it had to come to a decision on another fundamental issue, that of compulsion – should parents be compelled to send their children to school. *Laissez-faire* had long dominated economic and political thought, and there were many who viewed with abhorrence any government action that affected personal liberty. Members were reminded that there was compulsory education in the U.S.A., but the ardent libertarians alleged that in most of the states 'truantism and absenteeism were increasing every day'. Germany was also much quoted as an illustration of the successful operation of a compulsory system, but against this it was claimed that the historical and political background was quite different. Compulsion might work in Germany, it was argued, but it was 'something that England would never tolerate'. But, as the debates show, opinion on this subject was changing rapidly. There were strong humanitarian influences at work, and thoughtful people were shocked by the grim reality of the thousands of neglected children running wild in the streets of the large towns. There were, too, some useful precedents for compulsory education to be found in the Factory Acts, beginning with the Act of 1833: and in this country we usually take more kindly to a reform if it can be shown to be not quite new.

Perhaps more important was the impact on opinion of great reforming spirits like Matthew Arnold, Charles Kingsley, Carlyle, and, most influential of all in swaying liberal thought, J. S. Mill who in 1870 was at the height of his power. Although brought up to believe the full doctrine of *laissez-faire*, Mill came to realize that social justice could not be achieved unless one recognized that there are situations in which state action is imperative. While he had no faith in state education, regarding it as 'a mere contrivance for moulding people to be exactly like one another', he was convinced that parents have no right to deny their children the benefits of education. But at the same time he insisted that, in administering compulsory education, the greatest care should be taken not to impose on children religious teaching at variance with their parents' wishes. The 1870 Act often reflects views that Mill expounded so clearly: and one can see his influence in its sympathetic attitude to parents' consciences, and in Parliament's acceptance of the principle of compulsion with the emphasis not on attending school but on ensuring that all children have the opportunity of being educated at least up to an approved minimum standard. Compulsion came in stages partly because sufficient school accommodation was not at first available. The 1870 Act permitted school boards to introduce compulsion by by-law, but it was not made general until 1880.[1]

The foundation of the compromise was a dual system of voluntary schools belonging to various religious bodies, and board schools provided by local authorities (school boards) which were entrusted with the task of 'filling the gaps' left by the religious bodies. Supporting this dual system were important provisions designed to ensure that parents' wishes about religious education were respected. One was a 'conscience clause', asserting that no attendance at any place of worship or Sunday school nor any religious teaching or observance should be imposed upon any child if his parents objected. With the intention of making it less embarrassing for a child to absent himself from religious lessons a clause – afterwards known as the time-table clause – was added to the Bill during the debate which stipulated that the religious teaching should be given either at the beginning or the end of a session.

A still more important amendment – known after its sponsor as the Cowper-Temple clause – laid it down that no religious catechism or distinctive formulary should be taught in any Board School. School Boards were empowered to authorize 'simple Bible teaching' in their schools or, if they preferred, they could omit religious teaching entirely. All but seven School Boards in England arranged for Bible teaching to be given, but in Wales forty-three arranged for secular teaching only to be given, a decision attributable largely to the strength of the Sunday school movement in the Principality.

The compromise has proved durable. Modified and expanded, the dual system is still the basis of our law of education. The provisions safeguarding conscience remain on the statute book

1. For a fuller account see W. O. Lester Smith, *Compulsory Education in England*, UNESCO, 1951.

with the exception of the time-table clause which was rescinded in 1944 to release religious education from its irksome strait jacket. Of the decision in 1944 to continue the dual system and reshape it to meet modern requirements, Lord Butler has said,

no single step would have made or would make the education service simpler or tidier than to transfer voluntary schools to the ownership and total control of the State or local education authorities. But simplicity and tidiness are not the relevant criteria, and few steps would have been, or would be, more stupid. The Churches have a claim before history to a continued honourable role in English Education.[1]

Parliament in 1959 once again reaffirmed its faith in our dual system when in an Education Act of that year it agreed to an increase from 50 to 75 per cent in the rate of grant for voluntary school building; and in 1966 there was a further rise to 80 per cent.

CONFLICT OR COOPERATION

The 1870 Act produced schools but it did not bring peace: the school boards and the voluntary school managers coexisted in unfriendly rivalry. The next great Education Act, of 1902, to which reference will be made later, proved even more controversial: so much so that when Fisher drafted the measure that became the Education Act, 1918, he deemed it wise to exclude aspects that might arouse ill-feeling and jeopardize his Bill. 'Any attempt,' he wrote, 'to revive the fierce controversies of that memorable debate [1902] would have seriously impaired the cohesion of the Government, and wrecked such chances as I might have of making a useful contribution to educational progress.'[2]

Happily our other great Education Act, that of 1944, reached the statute book after a comparatively calm voyage: and this in spite of the fact that it dealt with the issues that Fisher deliberately avoided, especially the reconstruction of the dual system. Several factors contributed to this remarkable achievement – a very

1. *Jubilee Lectures*, Evans, for the University of London Institute of Education, 1952, p. 46.
2. *An Unfinished Autobiography*, p. 95.

outstanding President of the Board of Education; the valuable partnership of Lord Butler, the President, with Mr (later Lord) Chuter Ede, the Parliamentary Secretary, whose wisdom was matched by his wide knowledge of local government and of the teaching profession; the statesmanlike tolerance of William Temple, the Archbishop of Canterbury; a growing sense of unity among the Churches; Coalition Government; and the mood of Parliament and people, war-weary and yearning for a better kind of world.

The moderation and goodwill shown by our legislators on this occasion set a good example: and many were encouraged to hope that henceforward, both at the centre and locally, education would no longer be a subject of faction and intrigue. Mr Daniel Lipson, an M.P. who had fought a clean fight on behalf of the doomed Part III authorities,[1] voiced a general feeling when, during the concluding stages of the debate on the 1944 Act, he paid this tribute to Mr Butler and Mr Chuter Ede. 'It has,' he said, 'been a remarkable combination of Minister and Parliamentary Secretary, and I would express the hope that, as we have seen a combination of members of different parties producing a Bill of this kind, which is practically an agreed Bill, we may look forward to the time when education will be taken out of party politics.'[2]

THE CLAIM THAT EDUCATION SHOULD BE 'ABOVE POLITICS'

There are many who, like Mr Lipson, wish that education could be 'taken out of party politics', and certainly there is something incongruous about the intrusion of political warfare into a domain dedicated to the upbringing of children. But this 'hands off' attitude is scarcely consistent with our belief in parliamentary democracy, nor is it in tune with our democractic way of shaping policy by discussion. It is, however, a point of view sincerely held by a number of thoughtful people: and it is an opinion that appears to be gaining ground. It would seem, therefore, to merit more consideration than it usually receives.

1. Borough or U.D.C. responsible under Part III of the Education Act, 1902, for elementary education only.
2. *Parliamentary Debates (Commons)*, Vol. 399, Cols. 2163-4, 11 May 1944.

Education and Politics

One reason why there are more people who want education kept free of politics is that today more are conscious of the harm that can be done when schools get involved in party strife, or are made to serve some dubious political purpose. Never before has it been so generally appreciated that schools and youth organizations can be used and exploited. Time has not obliterated the memory of how Hitler and Mussolini geared their nations for battle by indoctrinating the young with expansionist dreams and the worship of military prowess. But much has happened since then to demonstrate still further how ready some governments are to use education to mould opinion: we have seen it in different countries enmeshed in controversial politics with racial, sectarian, lingual, or other divisive features. In this country at present our political climate is fairly temperate, and education seldom runs into rough weather. There is an underlying unity of approach, but this does not prevent partisanship, either at Westminster or at the County or Town Hall, becoming at times fierce enough to arouse the resentment of those who feel that education should not be used as a party battleground.

Another factor of some importance in creating the 'above politics' attitude is that a good many teachers and thoughtful parents regard education as an end in itself. Influenced consciously or unconsciously by the great American pragmatist, John Dewey, they think that, as he maintained, 'the educational process has no end beyond itself; it is its own end'. Holding such views, they see education as a world of its own in which children are helped to develop their abilities with the growth of personality to 'full stature' as the main objective. It seems to them almost sacrilege when politicians and others, unfamiliar with the theory and practice of education, fulminate and dogmatize about the aims of education or about how it should be organized.

Dewey's influence, still strong, was in this country at its zenith between the wars: and in the nineteen-twenties his ideas about education were fashionable. Addressing an audience of teachers at that time Stanley Baldwin, then Prime Minister, commented on the wide difference between the worlds of education and politics. 'The primary concern of those who have such a sacred trust as you have,' he remarked, 'is the unfolding of the child's personality and not the victory of party.'[1] This distinction is one that many who teach, or are closely concerned with education, would emphasize: they regard education as an intimate, personal affair remote from the cut and thrust of the political arena.

Early in this century many teachers still ruled their class by fear, but today most of them take a personal interest in their pupils. This friendly relationship between teacher and pupil, much appreciated by parents, has had a marked effect on public opinion which is much more on the side of teachers than it used to be. Political action or controversy harmful to schools generally, or to a particular school, often arouses popular disapproval. Public appreciation of what is done for children in schools today is certainly a factor to be reckoned with when estimating the weight behind the claim that education should be above politics. This rise in public esteem has given teachers a much stronger position in the community. Twenty or thirty years ago they attracted more than their share of criticism and mistrust. Today they normally enjoy a large measure of goodwill and the strikes over salaries in 1970, though regrettable, roused a good deal of sympathy.

It is for such reasons easier and more pleasant to be a teacher now than it was, and there is more encouragement to take pride in a vocation that people value. Most teachers have a personal regard for their work, not unlike that of the artist or craftsman, and this makes them dislike interference, especially that of people unfamiliar with their problems. In many respects teachers today are generally more highly qualified than their predecessors were and, in this status-conscious age, they show a growing sensitivity about professional status. So, although many teachers might not agree that education should be 'above politics', there would be strong and widespread resistance to any political move that showed lack of respect for the profession or imperilled any of those freedoms that teachers cherish.

The belief that schools should be free from external interference is an important element in our educational tradition. 'The good schoolmaster,' wrote Thomas Fuller in the seventeenth century, 'is and will be known to be an absolute monarch in his school.' The great head masters who inspired the public-school

1. *On England*, Phillip Allan, 1927, p. 165.

revival in the nineteenth century were ardent exponents of this doctrine. They were adept at keeping busybodies at bay and the more combative of them, strong characters like Thomas Arnold or Edward Thring, could be extremely tough with governors or parents who did not agree with them. Within their ramparts these schools developed their own way of life. 'The society of a public school,' wrote Bishop Welldon, who was Head Master of Harrow at the beginning of this century, 'is a world in itself, self-centred, self-satisfied. It takes but slight account of the principles and practices which obtain in the world of men. It has its own laws, its own fashions, its own accepted code of morals.'[1]

The conception of 'school' as a corporate society is now pretty general in this country, although it would be misleading to suggest that schools within the state system have all the freedom that the independent schools prize. The Fleming Committee stressed as 'the most striking difference of all' between public and maintained schools the fact that the former are 'under the control of independent governing bodies', and there are some other notable differences.[2] But it would be no less wrong to discount the rich seam of independence in our general educational tradition, or to regard it as a monopoly of the public schools. Indeed, the conviction that schools can only thrive when untrammelled by intrusions and distractions is widely held and, like much else that the public school reformers fought for, has become part of our educational creed. It no doubt contributes to the dislike of political intervention in school affairs.

But of all the considerations advanced to support the claim that education and politics should be kept apart, by far the most practical is the importance of maintaining continuity in educational practice. Plans and programmes become unworkable if policy changes fundamentally whenever one party wrests power from another. Nor is the damage that can be done by electoral upheavals restricted to the administrative aspect; schools lead unsettled and uneasy lives when, as sometimes happens, their

1. Quoted by Sir Joshua Fitch in his *Thomas and Matthew Arnold*, Heinemann, 1905, p. 75.
2. *The Public Schools and The General Educational System*, H.M.S.O., 1944, pp. 43–4.

future hinges on the changes and chances of polling day in county or county borough elections. The sense of insecurity and uncertainty is intensified when an authority makes an annual practice of adjusting the membership of the education committee and that of governing bodies to reflect as nearly as possible the relative strength of parties in the newly elected council. A party that has triumphed at the poll can, during the post-election phase, be pretty drastic; 'we are the masters now' is an attitude that often appeals to party stalwarts at such a time, but it is not one that makes for the good government of education either at the centre or locally.

WHO ARE THE OBSTRUCTIVES?

Politicians are, however, often blamed for crimes that they have not committed: and those who resent their intrusions into the educational sphere sometimes attribute to them misdeeds for which others are mainly responsible. For example, it is often alleged that by party strife they delayed for many years the introduction of our national system, and that subsequently they have from time to time blocked the road of educational advance. The story of our educational legislation hardly bears this out. We have already glanced at the situation which led to the passing of the 1870 Act, and it cannot be said that it was party politics that bedevilled that memorable occasion.

So far from proceeding on narrow party lines Gladstone, W. E. Forster, and their ministerial colleagues put first the necessity of finding a solution to the inflammatory religious question, one acceptable to a majority, irrespective of party. The Liberal Party suffered grievously in consequence as Joseph Chamberlain, then a fiery young Radical, prophesied it would. After 1870 the fortunes of the Government immediately began to decline. 'Before that date,' Sir Robert Ensor notes, 'it had been popular as well as strenuous, backed by a majority in the country no less than in the House. But from then a change set in. The majority at Westminster remained, though nerve-shaken by adverse by-elections; but that in the constituencies continuously trickled away. The earliest weakening was due to radical and nonconformist disappointment over the compromise policy of Forster's Education Act. Forster's own constituents in Bradford carried a vote of censure on him at his first meeting after the Act was passed.'[1]

But if we absolve the party politician, we must look elsewhere for the controversialists who for so long prevented legislation. They were for the most part men of high principles who held their religious convictions so strongly that they could not even agree to differ. 'Religion, the keystone of education,' said a Victorian statesman,[2] driven desperate by their wrangling, 'is in this country the bar to progress.' These earnest educationists were the heart and soul of the pressure groups mentioned in the first section of this chapter, and Tenniel depicted them in *Punch* as 'The Obstructives', all busy quarrelling and thereby barring the road to education. The 1870 Act bypassed them enough to make legislation possible, but it did not scotch 'the religious question'. That became a burning local issue: the rowdy school board elections were, in G. M. Young's graphic phrase, 'spiced with sect'.[3]

There can be little doubt that when people want education divorced from politics they are thinking not of party politics only but also of the drum ecclesiastic that has so often disturbed the educational scene. Happily it is now seldom to be heard, and for this relief all who care for education are grateful and not least those whose duty it might be to beat the drum. Thus when the Education Act of 1959, which raised the grant for voluntary school building to 75 per cent, was in draft a Roman Catholic bishop welcomed it as a step towards taking voluntary schools 'out of politics'. 'Every political party,' he added, 'is weary of the continual campaign we have been waging for voluntary schools. We are weary of it, too, but we have to do it.'[4]

But it is when education becomes a party battleground that most resentment is caused: and that is what happened in the early years of this century during and after the passing of the Education

1. *England, 1870–1914*, p. 19.
2. Sir James Graham, Home Secretary in Peel's second Ministry.
3. *Victorian England: Portrait of an Age*, Oxford University Press, 1936, p. 117.
4. The Rt Rev. G. P. Dwyer, then Bishop of Leeds, as reported in the *Manchester Guardian*, 12 January 1959.

Act, 1902. The disputations, the manoeuvres, and the intrigues of that period have now passed into history, but they caused so much resentment in their day that ever since those who have wished education well have done their best to preserve it from the ignominies of partisan warfare.

THE EDUCATION ACT 1902 AND THE PARTY WARFARE IT EVOKED

The political history of the Education Act of 1902 is an important study for anyone exploring the problem of the relationship between education and politics. It is a long, complicated story and some of its significant features are open to various interpretations: it would be misleading, therefore, to give a summarized version, which is all that is possible here, so instead let us look particularly at aspects that provoked conflict.

It should, however, first be said that the Act in practice proved a good, workmanlike measure under which much progress was made. It effected two major reforms, one transforming the local government of education, the other buttressing the finances of the voluntary schools. The first abolished the school boards, and made the county and county borough councils the local authorities for both higher and elementary education; the second, while retaining the dual system, helped the voluntary schools to meet the burden of rising costs by subsidizing them not only out of taxation but also from local rates. They no longer had to bear any maintenance cost except that for the upkeep of the school structure.[1]

Many, irrespective of party, welcomed the assignment to the local authorities of responsibility over the whole field of education, other than universities. With the Board of Education Act of 1899, which established a central department with a similar educational range, England and Wales were now provided at last with a unified education service. 'This,' said Sidney Webb with

1. For information and guidance about the 1902 Act see: Balfour, *Educational Systems of Great Britain and Ireland*, Oxford University Press, 1903; Halévy, *History of the English People*, Penguin Books, Epilogue, Book 2; Lowndes, *The Silent Social Revolution*, Oxford University Press, 1937, Chapter V; Curtis, *Education in Britain since 1900*, Dakers, 1952, Chapters 2 and 3.

his socialist outlook, 'renders the Bill of 1902 epoch-making in the history of English education'; and Haldane, then a leading member of the Liberal Opposition, and afterwards Lord Chancellor in a Labour Ministry, risked the grave displeasure of his party by supporting the Bill because, in his view, 'the importance of developing the national system of education was so great'.[1]

The Bill had been drafted by Robert Morant, a great civil servant of the strong, forceful type, with a passion for efficiency. It was piloted in the House of Commons by Arthur Balfour, who became Prime Minister during the Bill's stormy passage – fifty-nine days of parliamentary time. It is doubtful whether it would have become law if he had not taken charge of it personally and handled it with consummate skill. The Balfour–Morant partnership was a remarkable one. 'Balfour,' says his niece and biographer, 'never inspired a deeper devotion in a subordinate, and the zeal of another never had more influence upon himself.'[2] It was, indeed, a strong combination, but the Opposition was formidable too with Lloyd George, a rising young Radical, eager for the fray. There was opposition, also, within the Cabinet: for Joseph Chamberlain, now a Unionist, was as a nonconformist hostile and had to be reconciled. And there was as well a powerful array of Free Church stalwarts outside Parliament, including the redoubtable Dr John Clifford, a strong-minded, vigorous Baptist minister.

It would be unfair to label the 1902 Act as a piece of party legislation. In making the county and county borough councils the local education authority, Balfour was but implementing a recommendation made by the Bryce Commission in 1895. It was, in fact, a reform that many thoughtful people, irrespective of party, regarded as urgently necessary. It was, however, also true that most Anglicans disliked the school boards and, as the Conservative party was mainly Anglican, it too desired their demise. The abolition of the school boards was, therefore, good party policy; and it was a policy to which Liberals were naturally opposed because these boards were a Liberal creation and were now esteemed by their nonconformist supporters who had

1. R. B. Haldane, *An Autobiography*, Hodder and Stoughton, 1929, p. 148.
2. Blanche E. C. Dugdale, *Arthur James Balfour*, Hutchinson, 1936, Vol. I, p. 320.

acquired a regard for the undenominational teaching given in the board schools.

There were over 2,500 school boards, and there can be no doubt that many of them thoroughly deserved to die. But the school boards in some of the larger and more populous areas, including London, had done well. It was success, not failure, that proved their undoing; and it was by being ambitiously enterprising and stretching their powers to the full that they made enemies. How the position of the school boards was undermined and the ground prepared for their abolition is a long and involved story. By a study of many contemporary documents Professor Eaglesham has shed new light on what had hitherto been an obscure phase in our educational saga, and in his scholarly book – *From School Board to Local Authority* – he recounts the various and devious ways in which the school boards were hustled to their doom.

His researches appear to have convinced him that politics and education should, as far as possible, be kept apart: and he notes with concern that today it is becoming more difficult than ever to prevent the intrusion of politics into educational affairs. 'Pressure of events,' he observes, 'appears to be giving ever-increasing scope to political decisions in such matters as school organization and selection for secondary education.' 'But,' he continues, 'if there are few fields in which politicians now have such great powers and opportunities lying to hand, there is none in which they are likely to do more harm. . . . It is, therefore, a problem of some urgency to make education as independent of politics as considerations of public finance will allow; for behind politicians, administrators, regulations and rules are six million children whose paramount need is expert, unbiased, liberal teaching.'[1]

The Tory efforts to undermine the School Boards were, however, as nothing when compared with the Liberal campaigning against the 1902 Bill and, when it became law, against the administration of the Act. Working in close association with nonconformist leaders, they concentrated their attack on the proposal to aid voluntary schools with rate money. Of the nonconformist leaders, Dr Clifford was the most vehement. One of his battle

1. *From School Board to Local Authority*, Routledge and Kegan Paul, 1956, p. 182.

cries was 'Rome on the Rates', and he contended that the powers behind the Bill were the same as those who had persecuted non-conformists of old by means of the iniquitous Clarendon Code. He seemed to overlook the fact that they had persecuted the 'Romans' even more severely.

The nonconformists had one important grievance which still rankles today. In about 8,000 parishes, mostly rural, there was only one school: and in these 'single school areas', as they are called, the school was usually Anglican. Lloyd George had himself received his early education at such a village school, and in speech after speech he condemned with fiery eloquence the injustices suffered by nonconformist children obliged to attend schools in which the influence of squire and parson was often dominant. The Bill, he urged, meant 'riveting the clerical yoke on thousands of parishes'. (During the negotiations prior to the passing of the Education Act, 1959, Anglicans suggested, as a partial remedy, that there should be Free Church representation on the management of these schools.)

The storm continued after the passage of the Act. A Passive Resistance League was established under the leadership of Dr Clifford, and its members, the more militant opponents of the Act, refused to pay their rates. They were prosecuted – there were altogether about 70,000 prosecutions – and items of their possessions were 'seized' and sold to defray the rate payment due from them. More serious, however, was the revolt of certain Welsh local authorities who, encouraged by Lloyd George – 'no control, no cash' was one of his slogans – withheld rate-aid from voluntary schools. The Conservative Government countered this move by passing a Default Act[1] which empowered the Board of Education to pay money direct to managers of voluntary schools and deduct it from the grant payable to the defaulting local authority.

But in time – generally speaking by 1906 – these resistance campaigns petered out. Passive resistance ceased to attract public sympathy: 'the spectacle of Dr John Clifford forcibly having his teapot sold' was no longer regarded as martyrdom.[2] 'Slowly the

---

1. Education (Local Authority Default) Act, 1904.
2. See Cole and Postgate, *The Common People, 1746–1946*, p. 455.

welter of controversy died down,' says Mrs Cruickshank. 'It is hard to forgive the fanatical extremists on both sides who had degraded national education to a miserable quarrel between Church and Chapel.'[1] Not only were people growing weary of the conflict, but it was also becoming apparent, as a result of the quiet, thoughtful administration of the Act by local authorities and their officers, that it offered opportunities of a much better provision of education than had been possible in the past. Eminent nonconformists like Scott Lidgett, who had intimate knowledge and experience of local government, saw that important advances could be made under the Act and they ceased to cooperate with their militant friends. But in Parliament the party strife continued.

The campaign against the Act had helped to unite the Liberal Party, and had put it in good heart for the General Election of 1906, when it won a sweeping victory. It had an undoubted mandate to amend the Act of 1902, and the new Government lost no time in trying to fulfil its pledges. Augustine Birrell, famous as an essayist and wit, was the first President of the Board of Education in the new Cabinet; and he soon introduced a Bill designed to abolish the dual system. Local authorities were, under its terms, to be empowered to take over all voluntary schools; but these schools were to be allowed 'facilities' – either 'ordinary' or 'extended' – for denominational teaching. After consuming fifty parliamentary days, the Bill was destroyed by wrecking amendments in the House of Lords. Another unsuccessful attempt to modify the 1902 Act was made by McKenna, when President in 1908 : and later in the same year, yet another President of the Board, Runciman, tried and failed. This time the Opposition was – and who could be surprised – supported by the teaching profession 'who resented the fact that education was becoming the sport of party politics'.[2]

Of these abortive measures, the first was the most constructive, bearing promise of a unified system not unlike that in Scotland: indeed it has been well said that 'in the history of English education the Birrell Bill is unquestionably the great missed oppor-

1. *Church and State in English Education*, Macmillan, 1963, p. 88.
2. S. J. Curtis, *Education in Great Britain since 1900*, Dakers, 1952, p. 40.

tunity of the twentieth century'.[1] In its ingenious attempt to do justice to voluntary schools, it anticipated the Butler Act of 1944: for it recognized that there are two types of voluntary school, (*a*) the moderately denominational, and (*b*) the strongly denominational or 'atmosphere' school. For (*a*) Birrell proposed 'ordinary' facilities for religious teaching, and for (*b*) 'extended' facilities. Commenting on this Lord Butler has said: 'instead of the "facilities" for the Church schools of Birrell's Bill, my friends and I invented Controlled and Aided Schools'.[2]

Brief and inadequate though this sketch of the controversial background and acrimonious aftermath of the 1902 Act is, it is sufficient to demonstrate how education can be ill-used in the rough and tumble of party politics. In his autobiography Lord Morrison of Lambeth refers to 'the acerbity of political leaders' in the nineteen-twenties. 'There were no holds barred,' he writes, 'and the gentlemen who predominated in the control of the nation's affairs were capable of very ungentlemanly conduct.'[3] Education got involved in this unpleasant kind of political warfare rather earlier in the century being, as we have seen, a principal battleground during the first ten years of the century. Happily religion is not the dynamite that it then was, but there are other educational issues today scarcely less explosive; and it is noticeable that education is figuring more and more divisively in party programmes. Let us hope, however, that when in the years ahead controversial aspects of educational policy have to be decided they will be dealt with in the amicable spirit of 1944, and not as an occasion for party warfare.

THE NECESSITY OF POLITICS

This question of the spirit in which educational affairs are dealt with is all important. However strong the desire to divorce education from politics, it cannot be done; for, as the Greeks so clearly appreciated, education and politics are inextricably interwoven – about an eighth of Aristotle's *Politics* is devoted to

1. M. Cruickshank, *Church and State in English Education*, p. 103.
2. In Foreword to *Church and State in English Education*.
3. *Herbert Morrison: an Autobiography*, Odhams, 1960, p. 90.

education. As T. S. Eliot has said, 'one would indeed be surprised to find the educational system and the political system of any country in complete disaccord'.[1] We cannot, therefore, reasonably expect politicians to renounce their interest in education but we can appropriately hope that when dealing with it they will conduct their deliberations in the 1944 spirit.

'Politics are about power,' it has been well said, 'we cannot evade that truth or its consequences.'[2] And one of its most important consequences is that education, being a great formative influence and, as such, a vital source of power, must inevitably from time to time be a proper subject for political debate and action. The discussion will not necessarily follow party lines: there are, for example, staunch supporters of voluntary schools on both sides of the House of Commons. But there are educational issues about which opinion conforms pretty closely to the party alignment. For example, politicians of the Right tend to believe in the value of an élite and to stress the importance of training for leadership; and they are therefore naturally inclined to support public schools and grammar schools. While the more egalitarian Left are, as one would expect, usually opposed to separation at the secondary stage and often want all boys and girls in a neighbourhood to grow up together in common or comprehensive schools. This is an issue that, in some form or another, is likely to figure prominently in the political arena during the next few years: it seems to have taken the place of religion as the principal rift in the educational lute.

Such big political issues must be discussed, and our party system has grown up partly in response to the need for a public consideration of opposing opinions. The parties do not, as we have seen, always conduct their controversies temperately: but under wise leadership wide differences of opinion are often resolved harmoniously and effectively. We should not minimize the good features of our party system as a mode of democratic government. 'The system,' Professor Wilfred Harrison reminds us, 'has not operated on the basis of everyone insisting on maximum demands or

1. *The Idea of a Christian Society*, Faber, 1939, p. 36.
2. Sir Denis Brogan in preface to B. de Jouvenel's *Power*, Batchworth Press, revised ed. 1952, p. 12.

refusing to cooperate. We do not wish to excommunicate one another: we would rather sacrifice something of what we want and hold the community together than insist on what we want to the point of disrupting the community.'[1] Generally speaking, in our society the man with the reconciling mind is esteemed more than the ardent controversialist.

Conciliation usually requires patience: and sometimes, to achieve agreement, it is necessary to advance by stages. 'Very often,' it has been said, 'the majority opinion, which naturally believes itself to represent progress, has to administer its medicine in homeopathic doses. Hence the "time-lag", so exasperating to the reformer who has no doubts about the efficacy of his policies.'[2] But the wise educational reformer, even though it means some delay, will have regard to the views of his opponents. For vigorously rushing a debatable proposal through Parliament or Council by the use of a majority vote is likely, as in 1902, to intensify opposition and provoke counter measures.

One reason why education comes so much into the political arena today is that in a modern society planning is important. In education, as in other services, formidable powers are vested in the Secretary of State, and he is expected to put up a perpetual fight in the Cabinet and elsewhere to secure for education a good place in the Government's programme and in the allocation of priorities. It was for such considerations that Parliament and the country so readily agreed to the provisions of the 1944 Education Act that give the Minister an almost absolute authority, subject to Parliament, in the conduct of educational affairs.

Another consideration, argued at the time, was that a reasonably even standard of education throughout the realm could not be achieved unless the Minister was empowered to insist on similar standards of school provision in all areas. While it may be that one or two Ministers of Education have, on occasion, thrown their weight about unduly, it cannot be said that any have made a practice of using their powers immoderately. But it is important to remember that the Minister (now the Secretary of State) possesses great power and to remember, too, that the

1. *The Government of Britain*, Hutchinson, 1957 ed., p. 17.
2. C. K. Allen, *Democracy and the Individual*, Oxford University Press, 1943, p. 49.

sphere in which he operates is one of vital importance to us and our children. What is power? Lord Russell defines it as 'the production of intended effects', and he warns us that it is essential for our well-being for it to be 'widely distributed, and that subordinate groups should have a large measure of autonomy'.[1] In its important chapter on 'Academic Freedom' and its scope, the Robbins Committee stresses the necessity of autonomy for institutions of higher education: and it may well be that secondary and primary schools within the state system should be accorded much more independence. Certainly we need to think more than we have done about ways of counterbalancing the growing authority at the centre.

THE VALUE OF DISCUSSION

As education has strong political implications, it is sure to arouse controversy from time to time, reaching gale force when passions are stirred and the storm beats high. But, however stormy, few of us would wish to see the debate restricted, for we have been brought up to believe that the right of unfettered discussion is one of the most precious of our traditional freedoms. Hence our liking for Milton's famous words: 'Give me the liberty to know, to utter, and to argue freely according to conscience, above all liberties.' While it is true that education has suffered grievously from some past controversies, it is doubtful whether it would be good for education if its problems never provoked a storm or threw politicians into a ferment. 'When a thing ceases to be a subject of controversy,' says Hazlitt, 'it ceases to be a subject of interest.'

Discussion, controversial or otherwise, is an important feature of modern democratic government: its scope is widening and its influence on public opinion is increasing. Broadcasting stimulates it, and so does adult education in its many forms. We must, therefore, assume that education, whether we like it or not, will be more and more discussed; and, if it is a good discussion, is it not reasonable to hope that education will benefit? It is by talk and argument that policy takes shape, and some of the most

1. *Power*, Allen and Unwin, 1946 impression, pp. 35, 305.

important discussion procedures are part of the machinery of government. Thus discussion is a principal function of Parliament, of the Cabinet and its committees, of the party system, and of the electorate.

Departmental and similar advisory committees are also centres of discussion and their reports – as for example, the Crowther Report *15 to 18* and the Robbins Report *Higher Education* – promote discussion and furnish weighty material for it. Local authorities also provide a forum for debate, and education is frequently discussed by county and county borough councils as well as by their education committees. While outside the frontiers of the state there are innumerable societies, both great and small, which discuss public affairs and sometimes organize political pressure. Of these some are particularly concerned with education: and among the giants are the churches, local authority associations, and teacher organizations. There are many other bodies that provide opportunities for the discussion of educational policy: some of the most useful discussions take place under the auspices of radio (sound and television), the Press, and in courses (residential and non-residential) organized as adult education.

Discussion not only helps to shape opinion but it is also a recognized method of preparing the ground for an advance. The reports of Royal Commissions, Advisory Councils, and Departmental Committees, which are themselves the outcome of prolonged collective deliberation, focus attention on particular problems and set in motion constructive discussion on a wide front. Usually such bodies are constituted by the Government of the day or by a Minister to examine some problem that is causing concern; and Ministers are sometimes accused – often most unfairly – of using them as a convenient device for postponing action. When a Commission or Advisory Council presents its report, the political parties may adopt different views about the recommendations, or they may vie with each other in their urgent acceptance of the proposals. Some will say that it is good that politicians should take a lively interest in reports like those of Crowther and Robbins: how else can we expect their implementation? But there are others who resent the use of such fine reports as fodder for partisan warfare.

Much depends on the way in which advocates of debatable policies pursue their case. It was Plato's view that only those should be politicians who believe there is a life better than politics.[1] Politicians of that quality, when discussing educational issues, are unlikely to arouse the antagonism of those who care deeply for education. It is the lesser breeds, that in national and local affairs sometimes kindle resentment, and make people feel that education is being basely used as a pawn in the party game. Expounding the essentials of good democratic government and especially 'its method of discussion', Sir Ernest Barker emphasized the importance of 'a proper tone and temper of action'.[2] It is when educational controversy is conducted aggressively or for party purposes that resentment is most often aroused.

Party zeal, especially at election time, can stir bitter feelings that rankle and persist. 'As all politicians know,' observed a great historian who was also a politician, 'the desire for an attractive programme and a popular election cry is one of the strongest in politics; and as they also know well, there is such a thing as manufactured public opinion and artificially stimulated agitation. Questions are raised and pushed, not because they are for the advantage of the country but simply for purposes of party.'[3] When education figures prominently in rival election manifestos, there is ground for anxiety: it is gratifying to find such interest in education but this is offset by the feeling that some candidates will be unable to resist the temptation to use it as a party battlefield.

Ernest Barker maintains that for government by discussion to work successfully three axioms must be accepted and faithfully observed – agreement to differ, the rule of the majority, and compromise. 'If', he contends, 'majority rule is combined with agreement to differ and compromise, there will be no tyranny by the majority.'[4] In his view it is vital in our type of democracy that the majority should treat minorities sympathetically. 'As soon

---

1. *Republic*, 347. Quoted by Dorothy Emmet in *Function, Purpose, and Powers*, p. 121; she comments 'We distrust the politician who is only a politician.'
2. *Reflections on Government*, p. 34.
3. Lecky, *The Map of Life*, p. 164.
4. Ernest Barker, op. cit., p. 70.

as any political party,' he observes, 'begins to believe that it is the sole possessor of an exclusive truth, democracy is already dying or dead.'[1] If government by discussion is to prevail, educational policy should never be changed radically either at the centre or locally or for a particular institution without adequate consultation with those mainly concerned. While it will not always be possible to satisfy minority opinion, it should be considered patiently and with respect.

The story of how the Education Act, 1944, was framed provides a classic example of government by discussion at its best. It begins during the darker days of the Second World War when an attenuated Board of Education issued from its evacuation quarters a remarkable booklet in a green cover, entitled *Education after the War*.

This green book of theirs . . . saw the light fairly early in 1941: a confidential statement drawn up by the Board's principal officers, over a thousand copies of it were distributed privately to various organizations in such a blaze of secrecy that eventually, in response to demands in and out of Parliament, it was decided to issue publicly a summary of the main subjects and questions covered by the memorandum.[2]

It raised almost all the big questions that had to be resolved before a major Education Bill could be drafted and it stimulated the preparation of constructive replies by many organizations and individuals. It also formed the basis of discussion in many places, and not least in the Army in groups fostered by the Army Bureau of Current Affairs.

Soon after the circulation of the Green Book, Mr R. A. Butler was appointed President of the Board of Education, and from then onwards he, Mr Chuter Ede (Parliamentary Secretary), and Sir Maurice Holmes (Permanent Secretary) were busily engaged in sounding opinion, formulating and reformulating proposals, and interviewing innumerable deputations, representative of various interests. For considerations of space it is impossible to give a detailed account here of the prolonged negotiations, but when the Education Bill eventually became law the tributes paid were

1. ibid., p. 70.
2. W. O. Lester Smith's *To Whom Do Schools Belong?*, Blackwell, 1942, p. 155.

almost as enthusiastic about the way in which the ground had been prepared for its acceptance as they were about the legislation itself.[1]

This comment by *The Times*, made when Mr Butler had triumphantly brought his precious cargo safely into port, admirably reflects the contemporary view of his achievement:

By dint of unwearying patience and immense resourcefulness in negotiation, he produced a policy which provided for the complete recasting of the educational system, and yet at once commanded the widest measure of approval from Parliament and the Public. Circumstances favoured him, it is true. There was a general, keen desire for large-scale educational advance. Nevertheless, the unhappy history of educational legislation in this country served to throw into bold relief the greatness of his achievement. Undaunted by the fact that almost every Education Bill in this country for the past hundred years or more had been frustrated by denominational controversy or strife over the instruments of local administration, he boldly tackled both problems, and wove settlements of each into the greatest measure of educational reform the country has ever known.[2]

1. There are several good accounts of the negotiations but that in Chapter 7 of Dr M. Cruickshank's *Church and State in English Education* was written with the advantage of Lord Butler's information and advice.
2. *The Times*, 8 April 1944.

CHAPTER 5

Some Social and Economic Influences

EDUCATION AND SOCIETY

THERE are two principal ways in which schools can influence society. They can help to transmit what is good in our culture and perpetuate values that our forefathers rightly cherished. They can also be a creative and constructive force, improving the pattern and raising the quality of our society. Nor do these formidable tasks of conserving and creating attitudes rest only on the schools. Universities, colleges, adult education courses, broadcasting, the Press, and the family share this responsibility, and so do the churches. But schools have an unique opportunity of influencing society because, with rare exceptions, we all spend our most formative years under their spell. Characteristically we leave it to the head teacher and staff of each school to decide what use to make of the opportunity.

Remembering how bitterly teachers suffered in the past from the intolerance of 'the licence' and other oppressive devices, we rightly attach great importance in this country to academic freedom; and the Ministry of Education has been content in all matters affecting the curriculum and methods of teaching to do no more than offer guidance to teachers by means of 'suggestions'. The 'suggestions' are usually conveyed in pamphlets on different aspects of education or passed on by H.M. Inspectors during school visits or at teachers' courses. There is now a representative Schools Council for the Curriculum and Examinations that stimulates research and makes available to teachers in primary and secondary schools new knowledge on which to base their decisions about curriculum development and methods of teaching.[1] It has been careful not to encroach upon existing

1. See *The New Curriculum*, a Schools' Council publication, H.M.S.O., 1967.

freedoms, and it is now generally appreciated that if education is to have an effective role in shaping the new society and furthering the economy there must, in this age of planning, be from time to time clear guidance and bold leadership from the centre. There should be, too, a steady growth in the number of in-service courses and in the provision for postgraduate study. For we cannot in these competitive days afford long time-lags in the use of new knowledge, or in meeting new demands (for example, far more technicians, more teaching of modern languages), or in tackling some of the urgent problems of a changing society.

How to plan without sacrificing essential freedoms is one of the major issues of our time, and it is one that closely concerns education. There has been a good deal of planning in the educational field since 1944, and it has been accomplished without any obvious inroads on liberties that we cherish. But so far planning has been mainly in connexion with building programmes, and the curriculum – a more sensitive problem – has not yet received much attention at the ministerial level. All who value academic freedom will watch developments in this sphere with some anxiety, but if action from the centre still takes the form of guidance and suggestion there is much to be said for more leadership about what should be taught and about new aids and new methods.

If administered sympathetically, a system offering more guidance about the curriculum need not detract from the freedom that teachers now possess. Nor need it foster an undesirable uniformity: on the contrary, it could help to promote experiment in new directions and lead to more diversity than there is at present. 'While we have nothing like the uniformity to be found in countries where the curriculum is prescribed, there is, however, an underlying unity. Visitors from overseas, when they notice several schools of the same type with much the same time-table, often express surprise and even doubt whether our teachers are as free in this respect as they are reputed to be.'[1] Among the several factors that help to bring about these similarities, an important one is the impact of public opinion. 'An English School,' observed the Spens Committee, 'which departs widely from average prac-

1. Lester Smith, *Education*, Penguin Books, 1964 ed., p. 170.

tice can do so only with the support of a body of parents of unusual views.'[1]

Even more difficult than the question of guidance about the curriculum is that of advice from the centre about character training. Most people would agree with Plato that schools should aim at producing good citizens but, as the Ministry observes in one of its wisest pamphlets, 'the simple looking words, "good citizenship", raise some of the knottiest problems of politics, philosophy and religion'.[2] Somewhat surprisingly the law makes the local education authority largely responsible for seeing that children receive the kind of education that should make them good citizens. For it requires the L.E.A. 'to contribute towards the spiritual, moral, mental and physical development of the community by securing that efficient education is available' throughout the primary, secondary, and further education stages.[3] Fortunately it does not attempt to define the wide terms so freely used in this section and, in practice, the responsibility for character training has, like that for the curriculum, properly rested with the teacher.

How formidable a task character training is in the unsettling conditions of our time is well brought out by the Newsom Report in its excellent chapter on 'Spiritual and Moral Development'. After indicating some of the problems that confront a teacher trying to lay the foundations of good citizenship, it observes:

A school which takes its responsibilities seriously will not just leave to chance the working out of its influence over its pupils. It will have a policy and try to bring all its resources to bear.[4]

As with the curriculum, so also with character training, the question arises whether there should be guidance from the centre: and, if so, how and by whom the guidance should be formulated. Most crucial issue of all is the choice of objective. Thomas Arnold's achievement was largely due to the fact that he was quite

1. Report of the Consultative Committee on *Secondary Education*, H.M.S.O., 1938, p. 150.
2. *Citizens Growing up*, H.M.S.O., 1949, p. 6.
3. Education Act, 1944, Section 7.
4. *Half Our Future*. A Report of the Central Advisory Council for Education (England), H.M.S.O., 1963, p. 53.

clear on that point – his target was 'a Christian gentleman'; and it is probable that most of our schools today have a similar aim – such is the strength of the Arnold tradition – although it may bear various interpretations and differ as much from Arnold's version of 'a Christian gentleman' as does modern Rugby football from the game as first invented on a Rugby playing field.

There will be various opinions about the desirability of explicit guidance from the centre as to the kind of citizen that we should seek to develop; with us 'indoctrination' is an ugly word and the idea of 'conditioning' our youth is still more repulsive. But, as Sir Fred Clarke once observed, 'it is a profound error to assume that a free society, unlike a totalitarian one, is not concerned to produce by its educational methods a determinate citizen type'.[1] It is an issue that the thoughtful statesman cannot afford to ignore. Some educationists feel that we ought in our county schools to be more deliberate, less neutral, less non-committal in our approach to moral education. 'I believe,' says Professor Niblett, 'that we are not only thoroughly justified in biasing and influencing our children to have standards, to be courageous and believers in truth and freedom; it is our absolute obligation to do so. We must not be afraid of educating for commitment.'[2]

THE IMPACT OF SOCIETY ON EDUCATION

There are, of course, limits to what school and college can do in maintaining and improving attitudes and standards of behaviour. T. S. Eliot once reminded us of this, drawing attention to other influences, over which 'professional educators' have no control, that for good or ill profoundly affect our culture. He gave as examples the influence 'not only of family and environment but of work and play, of newsprint, and spectacles and entertainment and sport'.[3] Teachers are very conscious of these other influences which include some of their best allies and, also, some of their most dangerous and insidious enemies.

1. *Freedom in the Educative Society*, University of London Press, 1948, p. 9.
2. *Education and the Modern Mind*, pp 59–60.
3. *Notes towards the Definition of Culture*, Faber, 1948, p. 106.

Some Social and Economic Influences

Contemporary educational literature tends to concentrate rather gloomily on the influences in present-day society that militate against the good work done in schools. But it is easy to be too pessimistic and to underestimate the strength of the forces that are on the side of good citizenship. Schools can have no better ally than the good cooperating parent: and, happily, there are many households in which children enjoy an excellent upbringing. But more could be done, as part of our educational and social policy, to foster the good home and its cooperation with school. 'If the family is to be as secure in the future as it has been in the past (and we can be content with nothing less),' says the Crowther Report, 'there will have to be a conscious effort to prepare for it through the educational system on a much greater scale than has yet been envisaged.'[1] And it makes this – preparation for family life – one of its recommendations.

We are, perhaps, too inclined to forget our blessings. Consider, for example, our great good fortune that school broadcasting, from the empiric days of Mary Somerville onwards, has grown up under such good auspices to become the incomparable service that it is today. Then there is the School Health Service, which celebrated its jubilee in 1957: it, too, has a proud record, having with the School Meals Service transformed the physique of our children. 'School-children have the lowest death rates of the whole population, and this is the group which has gained most from the advance of medicine, especially public health.'[2] Remember, too, the many fine new schools – over 6,000 since 1944 – they are a great asset with their imaginative design, their spacious halls, light and airy classrooms, and attractive grounds. There are many other developments that are helping to create a more educative society, and among them TV (when it is good), community centres, village halls, adult education colleges and courses, an improving youth service, the Arts Council, school journeys, and much else.

1. *15 to 18*, H.M.S.O., 1959, Vol. I, pp. 37, 448.
2. S. and V. Leff, *The School Health Service*, H. K. Lewis, 1959, p. 3.

THE DARK SIDE OF THE PICTURE

There is, however, no ground for complacency. For as well as
the educative influences in our society, there are many that
hamper and undermine the good work done in school. What
happens to children out of school is so important a part of their
upbringing that it is rather surprising that those set in authority
over education do not give it more thought. 'It is,' observes Mr
Garforth, 'perhaps the greatest of our educational failures that
we have not understood the power of the social environment to
shape the character of the children. We have thus deprived
ourselves of a vital educational instrument and at the same time
frustrated much of what is done in schools.'[1] While the rural
areas have their problems, it is in the towns that the more disheartening features are usually to be found. Ours is a very crowded
island and, although there still remains some quiet countryside,
about 80 per cent of our people live in urban surroundings.
About two fifths of the population of the United Kingdom is
packed into the great conurbations around London, Manchester,
Birmingham, and Glasgow, and in Merseyside, the West Riding
of Yorkshire, and Tyneside.

Good homes are to be found everywhere, even in the most
derelict areas, but most will agree that the children and young
people who have the rawest deal are those born and bred in an
uncleared slum. Anyone familiar with the lay-out of big industrial
towns will know all too well those dismal inner districts that lie
half-hidden but quite close to the civic centre. Much of the
population has moved out to new housing estates, and only a
remnant remains. The children grow up in an environment of
mean streets and smelly alleys and live in squalid tenements,
spending their school-time as often as not in obsolete school
buildings sited on a narrow strip of asphalt, which they share
with antiquated outdoor lavatories, the caretaker's nightmare.
Tragic indeed are the deprivations suffered by children growing
up in such an area: often the 1944 Act is almost a dead letter and

1. *Education and Social Purpose*, pp. 86–7.

the situation is so grim that talk of 'equality of opportunity' has a hollow sound.

Professor J. B. Mays has put us all in his debt by making a special study of one such district, and he has made his investigation the basis of a book that should help to stir the public conscience. He describes in some detail the deprivations to which the children are exposed – emotional, physical, and intellectual. Only a few of them had reached a grammar school, and 'only one isolated individual from amongst many thousands had ever risen to the privilege of entrance to a university'.[1] The Plowden Report makes an urgent plea for 'Educational Priority Areas' following the line of the Newsom Committee which devoted a chapter to 'Education in the Slums' and recommended the appointment of a departmental committee to consider its problems.[2]

Such a committee, if established, would soon find itself involved in the difficult question of problem families. For they tend to live in areas where housing conditions are bad and the social environment depressing. Juvenile delinquency – that inexhaustible theme – would also figure prominently on the committee's agenda; for inadequate homes are the natural habitat of certain types of delinquency. Another item that would require thorough consideration would be 'child neglect', for that too is a characteristic of the problem family and of districts where the social environment is sub-standard.

One feature that such issues – problem families, juvenile delinquency, child neglect – have in common is that they do not lend themselves to generalizations. They are too personal. 'The time has passed,' writes Dr Harriett Wilson in her valuable study of a group of problem families, 'for speaking about "fundamental causes of delinquency"; we know they do not exist.'[3] But of the importance of the social environment as a basis for decent standards of behaviour there can be little doubt, and on humanitarian as well as educational grounds – if they are distinguishable – the case for a speedy end to slumland is overwhelming.

At the risk of digression let us here stress the need for good

---

1. *Education and the Urban Child*, Liverpool University Press, 1962, p. 186.
2. *Children and their Primary Schools*, pp. 50–67; *Half Our Future*, p. 26.
3. *Delinquency and Child Neglect*, Allen and Unwin, 1962, p. 24.

teachers in these dismal districts. As Professor Mays so truly observes, in such areas the school is often the natural centre to which the local people turn for help and guidance. 'School is their only sheet anchor.'[1] But, of course, the service that it can render depends on the quality of the teachers and on the staffing ratio. But, alas, while there are to be found in these areas some of our noblest and most devoted teachers, staffing is always an intractable problem and most teachers, not surprisingly, prefer service in more attractive neighbourhoods. Some picture the parents and children as rough and difficult, whereas more often, because of their hard lot, they are remarkably appreciative and responsive.

'It cannot be too strongly emphasized or too widely made known,' writes Professor Mays, '. . . that work in the older city schools is far from being the nightmare that many who have never experienced it believe it to be. Stories about indiscipline and general lack of response are all exaggerated.'[2] The Newsom Committee make a strong plea for the better staffing of these schools, urging that they 'require special consideration if they are to have a fair chance of making the best of their pupils'. 'They seem to us,' they continue, 'to need a specially favourable staffing ratio. Even more they need measures which will help them to secure at least as stable a staff as other schools. Perhaps this can be secured simply by making it clear that professionally it is an asset to have served successfully in a difficult area, and that work there can be intellectually exciting and spiritually rewarding.'[3] They also suggest the possible need 'for more tangible inducements', including residential accommodation near the schools because of the bearing of the problem 'on the whole life of the community'. But the appeal most likely to secure a good response is one stressing the urgent need for dedicated service in these desolate backwaters in which children are growing up without the bare essentials of a decent life.[4]

It is a relief to know that with the growth of slum clearance and rehousing, these blots on our urban landscape are gradually

1. *Education and the Urban Child*, p. 193.
2. op. cit., p. 183.
3. p. 24.
4. St Matthew xxv, 40.

disappearing. But many remain, and it must be admitted that when rehousing is achieved this often fails to bring about a much better standard of life. 'A new housing estate,' says the Crowther Report, 'if left without appropriate provision for communal life and adequate social leadership, can be as deadly as any slum.'[1] In the past we have tended too often to assume that when the houses and the schools have been built and serviced the authorities have done their part in creating a new neighbourhood. Various social surveys have, however, helped us to realize more and more that it requires a prolonged, persistent effort, and a disregard of frustrations, to convert a housing estate into an educative community. The task of repairing the social and cultural ruins wrought by the Industrial Revolution has, as yet, in many areas scarcely begun.

TOWARDS EQUALITY OF EDUCATIONAL OPPORTUNITY

The wide contrasts in social environment show that our chances in life continue to be largely dependent on where we are born and bred. This is one of the reasons why equality of educational opportunity is still little more than a dream. But it is certainly a great ideal, and since 1944 it has been an agreed objective of our educational policy, with the inevitable reservation that its full attainment is beyond human reach. It has for long been the ambition of social and educational reformers, and in late Victorian times it was earnestly discussed but as an academic rather than a practical issue. A good debating theme, it had zealous advocates, and some eminent opponents. Among the latter – to give an example – was Hastings Rashdall, philosopher, modern churchman, and a world authority on the history of universities. 'To give large masses of persons,' he said, after a lengthy examination of the proposal, 'an education which necessarily and inevitably awakens ambitions which cannot be satisfied, and tastes which cannot be gratified, and so to increase their discontent with that drudgery which must inevitably form a large portion of the lives of the majority . . . such a policy does seem to me, I confess, to involve a most gratuitous increase in the sum of human misery. And yet

1. Vol. I, p. 39.

that would be the inevitable result of a logical application of the principle of equality of opportunity.'[1]

There are still some who would reserve education of high quality for those deemed to be potential leaders, but the tide has turned strongly against them. In recent years we have been trying hard to provide all with a good education and, while much has been accomplished, we now know much more than we did in 1944 about the difficulties that have to be surmounted when striving to implement an egalitarian policy. Learning often by trial and error we have had from time to time to modify our views about what should be done and we have had to discard theories when they proved to be unworkable. For example, twenty years ago we made the mistake of accepting too readily some strange doctrines promulgated on Olympus about the organization of secondary education for all: for example, that human beings are of three main types; that one can tell to which type a child belongs when he is at the tender age of eleven; that Intelligence Tests are a sound instrument for sorting young children into these three categories; and that the I.Q. revealed at the age of eleven is likely to prove fairly constant. Methods of organizing secondary education are changing rapidly, largely as a result of the Labour Government's policy of ending selection at eleven and developing on comprehensive lines.[2]

To provide all children with a reasonable chance in education is, however, much more a social problem than an educational one. For injustices and anomalies in the social sphere leave their mark on our lives, especially during our formative years. As a result of their social surveys and other investigations the Crowther Committee were very conscious of grave social problems that impede educational advance. 'In every aspect of education,' they reported, 'and at every stage of our thinking we have been keenly aware of the way in which social conditions, attitudes and habits affect what education can achieve.'[3] In the previous section we touched upon the graver injustices done to children as a con-

1. *Ideas and Ideals*, Blackwell, 1928, p. 71. (The quotation is from an address given to the London Branch of the Christian Social Union in 1896.)

2. See the interesting Chapter 2 'Equality and Ability' in J. Vaizey's *Education for Tomorrow*, Penguin Books, 1962.

3. Vol. I, p. 36.

sequence of bad or inadequate housing, but there are several other handicaps, not so serious as squalor and neglect, that children suffer when housing is poor or unsuitable for their proper upbringing.

Some, for example, enjoy excellent facilities for doing their homework, while others find it well-nigh impossible to do it. 'Even when housing conditions are good,' note the Newsom Committee, 'large families and small living rooms, or the open-plan design of many modern houses and flats, may make it extremely difficult for boys and girls to have reasonable privacy and quiet in which to concentrate on their work.'[1] There can be no doubt that there should be the closest possible liaison between those responsible for the shaping of policy in education and in housing both at the centre and locally.

HOPES AND FEARS ABOUT MASS MEDIA

A very different influence in the upbringing of children and young people is that of the various 'mass media'. They can undo much of the moral teaching given in school and they can under-mine the efforts of teachers and youth leaders to encourage self-reliance and initiative. At their worst they give a new significance to St Paul's saying that 'Evil communications corrupt good manners.' They can, too, foster a dull, disheartening uniformity. 'More and more,' Professor Jeffreys complains, 'we look at the same things, listen to the same things, and passively receive the same services as they come off the conveyor belt of the Welfare State.'[2] On the other hand, these mass media have brought new interests into many lives, widened horizons, and stimulated thought. They are, indeed, bringing about such changes in human relationships that our outlook on life is undergoing a transformation.

'Already,' says Mr Raymond Williams in his fascinating book, *Communications*, 'some of our basic ideas of society are being changed by this new emphasis. From one familiar approach, through traditional politics, we have seen the central concerns of

1. p. 42.
2. *Personal Values in the Modern World*, Penguin Books, 1962, p. 51.

society as power and government. From another familiar approach, through traditional economics, we have seen the central concerns of society as property, production, and trade. These approaches remain important, but they are now joined by a new emphasis: that society is a form of communication, through which experience is described, shared, modified and preserved.'[1] Clearly this new force, growing in stature and strength, has, for good and ill, tremendous significance for education.

Of the good that it can do in the educational sphere broadcasting is an excellent example, while its power to harm is well illustrated by its exploitation of the young worker with money to burn. Too often (he or she) falls an easy victim to persuasion skilfully applied in the name of good salesmanship. 'Of all age-groups,' observes the Crowther Report,

the teen-agers are most exposed to the impact of the 'mass media' of communication. At school, they had the help of educated adults to enable them to distinguish and criticize; to master the suggestive and imaginative material put before them in a never-ending stream, and not to be mastered by it. As adults, they can hope to acquire a sufficient knowledge of life, a certain mastery in the art of running a home and earning a living, which will give them a touchstone for the vicarious experiences they get from screen or printed page. Most teen-agers have neither the one safeguard nor the other. They know they are not important as producers or as citizens. But their money is as good as anybody's. In their capacity as consumers, they get their fair share, and perhaps more than their fair share, of the attention of those who have goods or entertainment to sell; and though many of them are cynical enough about the reason for the attention they receive, who does not like being flattered? It needs, however, a very wise head to resist the suggestions of those who have to make their living by the correctness of their applied psychology.[2]

Housing and communications have one characteristic in common: they both concern education so closely that those responsible for the government of education should have a big voice in shaping their policy and practice.

1. *Communications*, Penguin Books, 1962, p. 10.
2. Vol. I, pp. 43–4.

SOME OTHER SOCIAL INFLUENCES

Those who govern education cannot ignore 'the tyrant custom'. In the Middle Ages it had something like the force of law: and in the realm of education, even in our unsettled society, it is often a decisive factor. When that wise interpreter, the late Sir Fred Clarke, returned to this country after years spent as a Professor of Education in Canada and South Africa, nothing impressed him so much as the strength of tradition in English education. His brilliant little book, *Education and Social Change*, was written to express his belief that, in spite of this respect for tradition, we could, if called upon, successfully adapt our educational system in order to meet the demands of a democratic society. We could do it, he felt sure, without losing what was good in our heritage. 'Like the wise householder in the Gospel,' he claimed, 'the English tradition can yet bring out of its treasure things new and old, and remain itself while putting forth new powers and transforming old organs to meet new situations.'[1]

He was, however, amused by some of our English attitudes to education. One that struck him as very odd was our habit, when discussing problems of secondary education, of leaving the public schools out of consideration. 'It is still true,' he commented, 'that the really important facts of English education remain for the mass in the region of the "taken for granted".' And he cited, an an example, the fact that the Spens Report, while directly concerned with secondary education throughout its whole range, did not discuss 'the leading secondary schools of the country'. 'The explanation,' he added, 'is, of course, not educational . . . but sociological.'[2] This evasive reticence continues. The public schools were accorded in 1942 their own Fleming Committee appointed by the Government in a too sanguine mood to 'develop' and 'extend' their association with 'the general educational system'. Now a Public School Commission under the chairmanship of Sir John Newsom is looking for ways of accomplishing what the Fleming Committee failed to achieve.

1. *Education and Social Change*, Sheldon Press, 1940, p. 2.
2. op. cit., pp. 9, 10.

Social class is still a big influence in determining the education a child receives. Those who consider themselves 'top people' usually send their children to public schools; members of the professions and executives are among the most ardent grammar-school parents; while those in the lower reaches of the socio-economic scale are sometimes apathetic about education of any kind. Statistics show that school leaving at fifteen – that is as early as permissible – is rare among the children of parents in professional and managerial positions, but still all too common among the children of manual workers. 'As one goes through the categories, professional and managerial, clerical and other non-manual, skilled manual or semi- or unskilled manual,' says the Crowther Report, 'the proportion of premature leaving at fifteen increases in that order, and the proportion of children staying on at school beyond the age of sixteen decreases.'[1] Great is the deprivation suffered by many of the individual children prematurely withdrawn by apathetic parents, and from a national standpoint such senseless waste of talent is indefensible.[2] But it should not be forgotten that while among the semi- or unskilled there are many apathetic parents, so too are there some who are the salt of the earth, as anxious as any that their children should have the advantage of all the benefits their schools have to offer.

A social characteristic of our time that militates against the proper upbringing of children and young people is the growing mobility of the population. The old Industrial Revolution was the cause of much uprooting, and our own industrial revolution is having much the same effect. Very few of us today live in the districts in which we were born. The settled, secure home life so usual at the beginning of this century has largely disappeared: and families often move more than once in the course of a child's schooldays, involving not only change of school but also parting with friends and the beginning of a series of new relationships. Only those who have experienced such disruption during child-hood can appreciate what such an upheaval means.

In 1901, out of England's forty counties, in only three were the

1. Vol. II, p. 18.
2. ibid., Vol. I, p. 453, para 671 (b).

natives less than 60 per cent of the population; by 1931 there were twelve counties in that position; by 1951 the number had risen to twenty. And one can change one's environment without changing one's county. How many people today are born and die in the same district, let alone the same street.[1]

And teachers are not the least mobile of our fellow-citizens. 'Of the teachers who were on the staff when the pupils entered the schools in 1958,' says the Newsom Committee, after examining returns for a sample of secondary schools, 'only half the women were still there in 1961, and about two thirds of the men. Not only had many new teachers come, but there had been a great many comings and goings in between.'[2]

Such frequent changes unsettle a school, creating restless, unstable conditions that are not conducive to progress. Nor in many areas is life out of school good for children; streets are busy and parks and play spaces are often some distance from home. Traffic increases and so do the perils of urban environment. 'Unfortunately modern conditions have introduced a new danger,' it has been said all too truly, 'and almost half the accidental deaths of children between five and fourteen years are caused by violence on the roads, now responsible for almost twice as many deaths as all the infectious diseases put together.'[3]

Education is affected, too, by another kind of mobility, one characteristic of a changing society: namely, the movement up and down the social escalator. The ambition to rise in the world is at least as old as Dick Whittington, and has never been so widespread as it is today. It has led to an intense, almost obsessional, interest in external examinations because they hold the key that unlocks the door into the universities, the technical colleges, and the professions and, thereby, to the seats of our meritocracy. This partly accounts for the bitter hostility to the eleven-plus because it was (and sometimes still is) the basis of a premature decision of profound consequence to a child's career. It also helps to explain why so many secondary modern schools present pupils for the G.C.E. and why there was

1. *15 to 18*, Vol. I, p. 43.
2. p. 11.
3. S. and V. Leff, *The School Health Service*, p. 3.

a demand for the establishment of yet another examination, one below the G.C.E. level.

Examinations with career implications were first used by the Chinese about three thousand years ago but here they cannot lay claim to any such antiquity, being an invention of our Victorian forebears, who had a liking for such measuring rods and believed that they promoted efficiency. It will be remembered that they introduced the objectionable system of 'payment by results' in the elementary schools, and it was again in the name of efficiency that they adopted the system of competitive entry into the civil service as recommended in the Northcote–Trevelyan Report. Trollope, himself a zealous civil servant, caricatures both Northcote ('Sir Warwick Westend') and Trevelyan ('Sir Gregory Hardlines') in *The Three Clerks* and makes fun of their unwelcome reforms. But, wrote Lord Iddesleigh, Northcote's grandson: 'Educationists, with whom Sir Stafford Northcote was very closely associated, gave the Report their strongest backing; seeing in its proposals an incentive to young men of promise.'[1]

Competitive entry as a method of recruiting civil servants soon proved itself a sound device, and, widely adopted for that purpose, it has led to a proliferation of examinations organized by professional and other bodies as a means of maintaining standards for diplomas or for admission. This generation, it has been said, 'accepts apparently without surprise and in general without comment the multiplication of examinations and diplomas in almost every conceivable human activity from Abbattoir management to Zymurgy'.[2]

Examinations organized mainly for schools followed a different course. They too began in the middle of the nineteenth century, the College of Preceptors leading the way. Schools appreciated them: they enabled them to compare their standards with those of other schools; a useful incentive, they were a spur to effort; they checked premature leaving; and they provided an acceptable credential when pupils entered employment or moved on to

1. In a Foreword to *The Making of an Administrator*, edited by A. Dunsire, Manchester University Press, 1956.
2. J. A. Petch, *Fifty Years of Examining*, Harrap, 1953, p. 13; see chapter 1 for an admirable account of the beginnings of public examinations in England.

institutions of higher education. So the demand for such examinations grew rapidly, and in response to appeals from the heads of grammar and high schools the universities somewhat reluctantly established examining bodies. The number of candidates for their examinations increased continually and some schools, proud of the results, developed the bad habit of presenting their abler pupils for several examinations. Dr Curtis, in his *Education in Britain since 1900* tells how he himself 'was entered successively for the College of Preceptors Examination, the London Matriculation, and the Oxford Senior Local'.

Fortunately H. A. L. Fisher, when President of the Board of Education, was able, with his strong academic background, to appreciate that these examinations mattered because of their influence upon the curriculum and their bearing upon university entrance and upon entry to the professions. Realizing that some control was necessary to end the chaos, he accorded a limited number of university-based examining bodies official recognition and they were made responsible for the School Certificate and Higher School Certificate examinations as they are now for the G.C.E.

His other administrative device was the establishment of the Secondary School Examinations Council, an advisory body which, with William Temple as its first chairman, soon proved its worth. It successfully kept watch and ward over the administration of secondary-school examinations, and after the Second World War played a valuable constructive role. Among reforms that it inspired were the transformation of the former School Certificate into the present G.C.E., and the provision of a new examination below the O level of G.C.E. (the Certificate of Secondary Education, C.S.E.) for the conduct of which special regional examining bodies have been constituted.[1] But this tendency of examinations to increase and multiply is surely regrettable. The work of the Examinations Council was transferred in 1964 to the Schools Council for the Curriculum and Examinations (see pp. 107–8).

---

1. See *The Certificate of Secondary Education; Notes for the Guidance of Regional Examining Bodies*, H.M.S.O., 1962.

THE NEW ECONOMY

Until recently our state system has been administered against a background of parsimony. The Victorian ideal was well expressed in the terms of reference for the Newcastle Commission (1858) – 'sound and cheap elementary education'. This was the aim of the system of Payment by Results and of the Elementary Education Act of 1870. Technical education, as a national service, also had an inglorious beginning. For its finance the Technical Instruction Act of 1889 was linked with the Local Taxation (Customs and Excise) Act of 1890; it provided 'the Whiskey Money' that helped the new county and county borough councils to aid technical education. The Education Act of 1902, which empowered the state to provide secondary schools, cost much more than its promoters thought it would. 'I did not realize,' Arthur Balfour admitted later to an eminent Socialist, 'that the Act would mean more expense and more bureaucracy.'[1] One of Balfour's main reasons for his slaughter of the School Boards was that the ambitious ones spent a good deal of money. 'I do not believe,' he said, 'that the system of an *ad hoc* authority with unlimited rating is one which really had any important experimental endorsement behind it.'[2]

During the inter-war years there were gleams of hope of a more generous outlook – the Fisher Act of 1918, the Hadow Report of 1926 – but, if there were sunny intervals, the clouds of financial stringency were always darkening the sky. Post-war depression wrecked the Fisher Act, and the Geddes Committee (1921–2) wielded its axe to such purpose that teachers' salaries were cut, the number of teachers was reduced, and as a consequence the size of classes increased. 'Frills' were sternly condemned. The May Committee set up ten years later to effect another pruning operation was shocked to find that the education provided by the state was sometimes superior to that provided in the private sector for the children of middle-class parents.

1. Halévy, *H:story of the English People*, Penguin Books, Book II, Epilogue, p. 123.
2. ibid., p. 123, note.

The attitude of economists to education has now completely changed. They have ceased to wield axes and, instead, have become standard-bearers of educational advance. Both Lord Crowther and Lord Robbins are distinguished economists, and no one who has read the reports of their committees could doubt the sincerity of their faith in the value of education both to the individual and to the nation. There is an interesting chapter in the Crowther Report, in which the point is made that traditionally in this country we have regarded education as serving two distinct purposes – first, 'the right of every boy and girl to be educated', and second, 'the need of the community to provide an adequate supply of brains and skill to sustain its economic activity'.[1] Both objectives, says the Report, are 'worthy and compelling', and it accepts them both. 'Primacy,' it continues, 'must be given to the human rights of the individual boy or girl. But we do not believe that the pursuit of national efficiency can be ranked much lower – not least because without it the human rights themselves will not be secure.'

So much are we under the spell of the economists today that we are inclined to discuss education in their language. In his *Education in an Industrial Society* Professor G. H. Bantock gives examples of this – in his view – 'disquieting use of language and terminology' that presents education as 'an investment', 'a commodity', 'untapped wealth', a source of 'qualified manpower'; and he says of the Crowther Report:

The impression one carries away from a reading is that it is the need for 'educated man-power' in terms relevant to the continuance of the 'affluent society' . . . rather than a deep concern for the human predicament in a materialistic and mechanical age that the committee consciously or unconsciously felt to be the really important aspect of their work.[2]

But it is good to have the economists on the side of education – there are good precedents for this, notably Adam Smith and J. S. Mill.

1. Chapter 6.
2. *Education in an Industrial Society*, Faber, 1963, pp. 86–7, 114, 179.

The economists have certainly done a great service by stressing the relationship between economic growth and education. In the past the solemn financial watchdogs used to demand their 'cuts' with confidence when education estimates showed an increase, and today they certainly can complain that the cost of education, expressed in money terms, is steadily rising. 'But,' says the Crowther Report, 'so has everything else, and it serves little purpose to quote ever mounting figures in pounds sterling. The only way to arrive at a true measure of the cost of education is to estimate what proportion of the total national income is represented by education – that is, what proportion of each year's total national output of goods and services is devoted to the educational system.'[1]

Education has for some time been getting a bigger slice of the national cake. In 1957 it took 4 per cent of the gross national product, if one includes what the Department calls 'related expenditure', i.e. welfare and other amenities related to the educational system – e.g. the costs of residential provision in colleges of education. By 1960 the percentage had risen to 4·3, and the provisional figure for 1968–9 is 6·2.[2] Much of the increase can be attributed to the remarkable increase in the number of students receiving 'higher education' (using the Robbins definition). The numbers have doubled within a decade. Among other factors are the movement of population and the educational needs of new housing areas.

Local Education Authorities pay for most of the education in the public sector, but they in turn receive grants from the central government that cover a great part of this expenditure. The proportion of the cost thus met by grant from the centre tends to increase. Professor Vaizey in his masterly book on *The Costs of Education*[3] has made some interesting calculations of the proportion of the cost borne by the central government. The proportions refer to total expenditure, including universities, for the whole kingdom. In 1920 the central government paid for 50

---

1. Vol. I, p. 56.
2. *Education Statistics for the United Kingdom*, p. 53 (H.M.S.O. 1970).
3. Allen and Unwin, 1958, p. 49.

per cent of the total, 8 per cent came from fees and endowments, and 42 per cent from the local rates. By 1955 the proportion of total expenditure financed from the centre had risen to 58 per cent, and local payments had fallen to 36 per cent. With the passing of the Local Government Act, 1958, the specific education grant to local education authorities in England and Wales was discontinued – the grant for school meals and milk is an important exception – and education was included among the services covered by the general grant paid to local authorities by the Ministry of Housing and Local Government. When this important change was made in the grant regulations many feared that education would receive less generous treatment, and that in some areas there might be a decline in the standard of provision for education. But so far education has not suffered noticeably under the new arrangement.

The changing attitude to education is due partly to our increasing prosperity. Governments can afford to be more generous, and parents can afford to let their children stay longer at school. 'As compared with our predecessors of the Consultative Committee who produced, in 1938, the Spens Report on Secondary Education, we are,' said the Crowther Committee, 'prescribing for a community that is one third richer in material wealth. This has a double implication: there should be more real sources available for education; and since a high level of national productivity can only be sustained by brains and skill the schools have a higher challenge to meet.'[1] The standard of living has greatly improved – compared with twenty years ago the consumption per head shows a value increase of about ten per cent; and, although there have been ups and downs in the employment situation, we have, generally speaking, been enjoying a period of full employment.

There has been an increasing demand for well qualified personnel, especially for scientists, technologists, and technicians. Qualifications are not, however, as durable as they used to be: new knowledge reaches the workshop with astonishing rapidity, and techniques and processes are constantly changing. Clearly adaptability is going to become more and more important: and

1. Vol. I, p. 45.

that means a good general education. But no less essential will be postgraduate courses and in-service training as a means of keeping up-to-date.

But qualifications are not enough for a useful and satisfying life in our changing society. For the revolution that is transforming science and technology is also changing standards and weakening the impact of tradition. In such a situation the character-training role of the school has, more than ever, a vital significance. To quote one who was revered for his wisdom:

> Where a social tradition is firm and effective, no great harm is done if the schools confine themselves in the main to teaching the distinctively school subjects. The influences which touch the deeper springs of character are supplied in other ways. Religion, tradition, the home, prevailing custom and the institutions of the national life all exert their influence on mind and heart. It is far otherwise when the social tradition is in a process of dissolution. It then becomes imperative that the school should assume wider functions and definitely set itself to the task of creating and fostering the sense of social obligation and loyalty to the community.[1]

THE IMPACT OF WARS

Big-scale warfare seems always in our modern history to lead to educational reform. Why this should be is a profound question, and for an answer we must look to those who have a special insight into our human nature. There are, however, three likely reasons. One is that a prolonged war serves as a kind of national audit: it exposes weaknesses ruthlessly and rouses a determination to make good the deficiencies that have been revealed. Another reason is that war smites the public conscience: there is remorse after the sacrifice of so many young lives, and a tortured humanity resolves to create for future generations a better kind of world. A third reason is that wars bring issues of power into the forefront, and serve as a reminder that education can be an important source of national strength. Or, as Sir Winston Churchill once declared, 'The future of the world is to the highly educated races.'

1. J. H. Oldham, 'Recent Tendencies in African Native Education', *Journal of Royal Society of Arts*, Vol. LXXV, No. 3888, 27 May 1927, p. 655.

One cannot, however, claim much idealism for the Newcastle Commission appointed during the aftermath of the Crimean War. But it was much influenced by the climate of opinion that that war helped to produce. The emphasis on 'cheapness' in its terms of reference was largely due to the fact that at the time the nation was sorrowfully counting the cost of this Crimean adventure: and the attention paid to 'efficiency' by the Commission is partly explained by the furore caused by the astonishing series of blunders that characterized this ill-starred campaign.

A few years later came the Franco–Prussian War and that certainly helped Forster to get the Elementary Education Act of 1870 accepted by Parliament. 'Germany,' said G. M. Trevelyan, 'who had conquered Austria in 1866, and was now engaged in conquering France, was in the forefront of all men's thoughts that year (1870), and she attributed her success to the schoolmaster as well as to the drill-sergeant.'[1] The war had not begun when Forster introduced his Bill but he, at once, struck a warning note about the dangerous forces mobilized on the Continent. 'Upon the speedy provision of education,' he urged the House of Commons, 'depends also our national power. Civilized communities throughout the world are massing themselves together, each mass being measured by its force; and if we are to hold our position among men of our own race or among the nations of the world, we must make up the smallness of our numbers by increasing the intellectual force of the individual.'[2]

Again and again during the debates members referred to the growing power of Germany and, towards the close when the Franco–Prussian War was raging, Forster spoke ominously of 'the terrible events transpiring around us in Europe'.[3] There were, too, in 1870 influential voices outside Parliament drawing attention to Germany's well-organized educational system and the way in which it had contributed to her unification and revival. 'In that fateful year,' Trevelyan reminds us, 'two books, Matthew Arnold's *Friendship's Garland* and George Meredith's

---

1. *British History in the Nineteenth Century*, p. 353.
2. *Verbatim Report of the Debate of the Elementary Education Act 1870*, published by National Education Union, p. 18.
3. op. cit., pp. 514–15.

Harry Richmond, warned England that national education and national discipline in the Teutonic heart of Europe was creating a new kind of power that had a jealous eye on our easily won, carelessly guarded, ill-distributed wealth.'[1]

Balfour's Bill of 1902 was also a war-time product. It was introduced in the House of Commons on the very day that the Boer War came to an end. Our generalship had not been our strongest asset in that long-drawn-out struggle; but, as Balfour's niece records, 'the disagreeable discoveries made by the British nation during the Boer War were not confined to the short-comings of our generals'.[2] Quite apart from its controversial aspect, the Bill aroused great interest and meetings held in the bigger towns, when it was under discussion, attracted audiences of about 5,000. Some of this enthusiasm was undoubtedly due to the disillusionment produced by the war and the consequent yearning for reform. Mr G. A. N. Lowndes who writes so well about the Balfour Act in his *The Silent Social Revolution* makes the comment: 'It would be an interesting study to trace how often in the course of the history of western Europe warfare, whether actual or economic, has stimulated interest in education.'[3]

To the Boer War we also owe the initiation of the School Health Service, the introduction of a School Meals Service, and many developments designed to raise the standard of national physique – for example, systematic physical education, open-air schools for delicate children, greater attention to personal hygiene and to the standard of school accommodation. For after that war, in which the brilliant guerrilla tactics of the Boers revealed many shortcomings in our soldiering, much attention was given to problems of national fitness. A committee was set up to inquire into physical deterioration in England and Wales, and for Scotland there was a Royal Commission on Physical Training. Their recommendations and their revelations about the physical unfit-ness of a high percentage of Army recruits led to the passing of the Education (Administrative Provisions) Act of 1907, which laid the foundations of what is now known as the School Health

1. *English Social History,* p. 557.
2. *A. J. Balfour,* Vol. I, p. 372.
3. p. 87.

Service, and strengthened the hand of the small Labour Party in securing the enactment of the Education (Provision of Meals) Act of 1906, the first legislative step towards a School Meals Service.[1]

War also created the opportunity for the Education Act of 1918. Becoming Prime Minister during a grim phase in the First World War, Lloyd George called H. A. L. Fisher from the seclusion of the academic world to become President of the Board of Education and to produce an Education Bill. With his customary shrewdness the Prime Minister had gauged the mood of the nation perfectly.

Men were deeply impressed by the tragedy and waste of war. Surely, from this sacrifice some great good must emerge ? Surely we must close our ears to the cynics who say that war merely breeds war ? So, against this background of loss and suffering, endured mainly by the young, the stage was set for educational reform.[2]

Fisher realized that there was no time to lose: the fervour of war-time might soon evaporate if peace came. 'The war was my opportunity,' he wrote later, 'I was sensible from the first that while the war lasted reforms could be obtained that would be impossible to realize in the critical atmosphere of peace.'[3]

His Act raised the compulsory school-leaving age to fourteen for all, thus ending the iniquity of half time, but his provision for a chain of day continuation schools throughout the country perished in the gloom of post-war depression. 'When we achieved victory and desired a new world,' said Lawrence of Arabia of those years of disillusionment, 'the old men came out again and took from us our victory, and remade it in the likeness of the former world they knew.'

The last of our great education statutes, the Education Act of 1944, was also, as we have already noted, essentially a war-time measure. Mr Butler's concluding words, when introducing it to the House, deserve to be remembered. 'Hammered on the anvil of this war,' he declared, 'our nation has been shaped to a

---

1. For a good short account of the attention paid to health and physique after the Boer War, see C. Birchenough, *History of Elementary Education*, pp. 194–8.

2. D. Ogg, *Herbert Fisher*, Edward Arnold, 1947, p. 63.

3. *Unfinished Autobiography*, p. 103.

new unity of purpose. We must preserve this after victory is won if the fruits of victory are to be gathered; and that unity will, by this Bill, be founded, where it should be founded, in the education and training of youth.' After the war came years of austerity, and Mr Butler, surveying progress eight years after the passing of the Act, observed: 'This is the irony of the Act of 1944. Though there have been real and striking advances, its full and rapid implementation is being retarded by the aftermath of that same war which called it forth.'[1]

Since then much has been accomplished, although two very important provisions of the Act have not yet been implemented – the raising of the leaving age to sixteen, and the establishment of county colleges. There has, however, not been the disillusionment that came after 1918 nor has the desire for educational advance weakened. There can be little doubt that yet another war, the cold war, has helped in recent years to secure for education more priority than it would otherwise have enjoyed; and in technical education, especially, the importance of matching as nearly as we can the achievement of other powers has been frequently stressed – for example, in the White Paper on Technical Education issued in 1956. 'From the U.S.A., Russia and Western Europe,' it warns, 'comes the challenge to look to our system of technical education to see whether it bears comparison with what is being done abroad. Such comparisons cannot be made accurately because standards and systems of education vary so much, but it is clear enough that all of these countries are making an immense effort to train more scientific and technical manpower and that we are in danger of being left behind.'[2]

1. *Jubilee Lectures*, Evans, for the University of London Institute of Education, 1952, p. 53.
2. Cmd 9703.

CHAPTER 6

Some Thoughts about Administration

THE MINISTER OF EDUCATION

ONE of the big reforms achieved by the 1944 Act was the appointment of a Minister of Education vested with substantial powers. Before 1944 – that is to say, under the Board of Education Act, 1899 – there was a President of a Board of Education, a body that never met: and its duty was defined as 'the superintendence of matters relating to education'. Very different is the role prescribed for the Minister of Education: he is required 'to secure the effective execution by local authorities under his control and direction, of the national policy for providing a varied and comprehensive educational service in every area'.[1] His powers are absolute, subject to, first, certain provisions in the Act; second, his general responsibility to Parliament; and third, his obligation to lay before Parliament rules he proposes to enforce. He makes known his requirements for the organization and administration of the educational system by means of statutory rules and orders, regulations and circulars. And he is empowered to overrule a local education authority or the managers or governors of any school within the state system if in his opinion they have acted, or propose to act unreasonably.[2]

These powers have, on the whole, been used wisely. 'No Minister,' says Professor Dent, 'has yet even attempted to use these powers dictatorially, and there would be a first-class political crisis if he did. Consultation and negotiation are the means he is expected to employ, and in fact does employ.'[3] It can be said, too, that the spirit of partnership between central and local government has survived the drastic shift in the balance of power. The

1. Education Act, 1944, Section 1.   2. Section 68.
3. *The Educational System of England and Wales*, University of London Press, 1969 edition, p. 65.

Ministry is, however, now indisputably the senior partner but there can be few, even in local authority circles, who would wish to curtail the Minister's rights of direction and control. For thereby he is able to deal with priorities, insist upon minimum standards, keep watch over staffing ratios, maintain some degree of parity in the scale of awards to students, and in other ways help to even out differences in the quality of schooling available in one locality or another.

The Minister can also do much towards ensuring that in the country as a whole adequate provision is made for particular needs where the demand is too small for the provisions to be made locally or regionally: for example, very special branches of technical education, or a school or schools for children suffering from some unusual disability. We have now over twenty years experience of this concept of a Minister armed with great powers, yet subject to some effective restraints, and it has proved itself a valuable device for the government of education. It could lead us, without much loss of liberty, far along the road towards the unattainable goal of equal educational opportunity. But, as the previous chapter shows, there are aspects of society that affect educational opportunity no less than do the branches of education for which the Minister is held directly responsible. 'To all of us,' Carlyle once said, 'the expressly appointed school-masters and schoolings we get are as nothing, compared with the unappointed, incidental and continual ones, whose hours are all the days and nights of our existence.'[1]

It may be that Carlyle, to emphasize his point, overstates the influence of 'out-of-school' as against 'in-school': but housing, health, mass media, and child neglect are all examples of 'unappointed' factors that profoundly affect the life chances of growing boys and girls. This suggests – does it not? that the Minister of Education should be an outstanding member of any Government, able to speak up to good purpose for education in the widest sense in all places where policy is being hammered out. There have been twelve Ministers of Education since 1944, and there was a period in the nineteen-fifties when the Minister was not even a member of the Cabinet. As a contrast, consider Plato's

1. *Life of Sterling.*

view: 'He who is elected, and he who is the elector,' he maintained, 'should consider that of all the great offices of state this is the greatest . . . The legislator ought not to allow the education of children to become a secondary or accidental matter. He who would be rightly provident about them, should begin by taking care that he is elected who of all the citizens is in every way the best . . . And he shall hold office for five years.'[1]

This question of the stature of the Minister of Education was brought into the limelight prominently by the Robbins Committee. For after a lucid and cogent exposition of the pros and cons it recommended the appointment of two Ministers – one to be responsible by means of a Grants Commission for universities and other autonomous, state-supported institutions, and the other to have much the same responsibilities as the Minister of Education has at present.[2] As soon as the Report was published there was prolonged argument in Parliament and the Press about this recommendation, the issue usually narrowing itself down to the question of: 'One Minister or two?' University opinion was generally in favour of the Robbins plan of two Ministers, but a great many, including some, like Lord Morrison of Lambeth and Viscount Eccles, with long experience of government, spoke strongly in support of a single Ministry.

Education greatly needs a spokesman of high calibre able to battle or mediate on its behalf whenever its interests – and they are wide – are at stake; and the need for a powerful advocate in the Cabinet cannot be over-emphasized. For such a role one Minister is obviously better than two, and this view was cogently and clearly expressed by Sir Harold Shearman in his Note of Reservation in the Robbins Report. Differing from his colleagues on this point, he put the case against 'Two Ministers'. 'What is to be feared,' he wrote, 'is that each will be fighting for his own hand and both may suffer. The impact of this situation in the schools, whose needs are and are likely to continue to be insistent, could be serious – particularly if one result should be that the Minister of Education were supplanted as a member of the Cabinet by the Minister regarded as responsible for the "senior" institutions'.[3] There

---

1. *The Laws* (Jowett's translation), Book 6.
2. Vol. I, pp. 246–52, 289.   3. Vol. I, p. 293.

were many, too, who thought that the Robbins recommendation was contrary to the prevailing tendency to coordinate and combine. And, as a recent example of this, the decision to unite the service departments under a single Ministry of Defence was much quoted. Fortunately, as indicated at the end of this section, the idea of 'One Minister' has prevailed.

The Minister of Education is required by law (Education Act, 1944, Section 4) to appoint two Central Advisory Councils (one for England, the other for Wales); and it is their duty to advise him 'upon such matters connected with educational theory and practice as they think fit, and upon any questions referred to them by him'. Usually their advice is confined to questions definitely referred to them, and among their recent reports are those popularly known as the Crowther and Newsom Reports, so called because Lord Crowther was chairman of the Council when the first was under consideration and Sir John Newsom when the second was framed. Such reports deal with problems that necessitate prolonged thought and investigation, including the hearing of much evidence by associations and individuals, and usually take about two years to construct. 'The great bulk of advice and assistance, given to the Secretary of State, comes, however,' says Professor Dent, 'from his Department, the Department of Education and Science. This is both his chief source of advice about national policy for education, and the chief means for securing that policy is carried out in practice.'[1]

The Ministry has a staff of about 2,700, of whom some eighty belong to the administrative grade, the grade mainly concerned with issues of policy. While of high academic quality, these civil servants do not necessarily devote their lives to education. Theirs is a mobile service: some come to 'Education' from other departments, while some leave 'Education' to serve some other Ministry. There are also in the Ministry of Education professional civil servants, including lawyers, architects, medical officers, and statisticians. And there are the inspectors, the H.M.I.s, over 400 of them; and one of their responsibilities is 'to act as the expert advisers of the Ministry on matters of educational theory and practice'. Such then is our modest Leviathan: no tyrant as yet,

1. *The Educational System of England and Wales* (4th ed., 1969), p. 74.

but occasionally high-handed and not averse to tightening its grip when given the opportunity. That is a natural process. 'Every established body of men,' Herbert Spencer once said, 'is an instance of the truth that the regulative structure tends always to grow in strength.'[1] We can be thankful that ours is a good Ministry, for its power has grown enormously in recent years.

With the appointment of an educational overlord this growth of power at the centre is likely to continue. After much deliberation the Government rejected the Robbins proposal for 'Two Ministers', and decided that there should be a single Minister with responsibility over the whole educational field and that he should be designated Secretary of State for Education and Science. Under him are two Ministers of State, one concerned mainly with the schools, and the other with institutions of university status. There was no substantial change in the responsibilities of the Secretary of State for Scotland for Scottish education, and the Scottish universities remain within the university structure for the U.K. and are financed through the University Grants Committee. It is a decision likely to have far-reaching consequences, and may well prove to be one of the great landmarks in our educational history.

THE COUNTER-WEIGHTS

It is, however, still true that the basis of our educational administration is a friendly partnership between the Ministry and local education authorities. 'If today the senior partner has a little more say than formerly and the junior partner somewhat less, the partnership still remains and each local education authority has a real measure of freedom and responsibility.'[2]

In fact, the law carefully provides for such a distribution of power and, as regards function, puts the stress on 'national policy' for the Minister and on 'effective execution' for the local authority. Admittedly the L.E.A.s have to operate under the

1. *Problems of Ethics and Sociology* (Quoted by B. de Jouvenel, *Power*, Batchworth Press, revised ed., 1952, p. 108.)
2. *The London Education Service*, London County Council, 1954, pp. 92–3.

Minister's 'control and direction' and it must be allowed that those crucial words have a not too respectable ancestry. For, as Professor W. A. Robson reveals, the phrase is borrowed from the Poor Law Amendment Act, 1834, 'under which the public assistance authorities were completely subordinated to the central department'.[1] But that should only intensify our vigilance, and put us on our guard against encroachments by the centre upon the L.E.A.'s traditional domain.

Local authorities have their critics, and among them some who are particularly well informed. For example, Dame Evelyn Sharp, armed with her experience as Permanent Secretary to the Ministry of Housing and Local Government, has on more than one occasion lamented some of their shortcomings, notably the declining quality of councillors.[2] Discussing in a leader some of her criticisms, *The Times* remarked upon

the demographic fact that people who might be expected to take part in public life – professional men, industrial managers and executives, for instance – tend more and more to have their place in a national career structure, often moving with each step in their promotion. They do not put down local roots.[3]

A survey, conducted by *The Times*, provides an impression of the occupational make-up of some Councils. The investigation covered twenty-nine city and town councils, and one county council. Of 2,230 council members, the numbers in the principal occupational groups were: retired, 283; housewives, 239; company directors, 165; trade-union officials, 68; solicitors and barristers, 63; builders and contractors, 52; estate agents and surveyors, 32; and doctors, 23.[4] Note the strong preponderance of retired people and housewives and the absence of teachers.

Active membership of an Education Committee, and especially as Chairman of the Committee or a standing sub-committee, often involves almost full-time service. This makes it impossible for many public-spirited people to serve, and in this respect local government is faced with much the same problem as Parliament.

1. *British Government since 1918*, Allen and Unwin, 1950, p. 130.
2. e.g. in addresses to the Rural Life Conference of the National Council of Social Service (20 July 1958) and to Association of Municipal Corporations, 22 September 1960.
3. *The Times*, 23 September 1960.   4. *The Times*, 9 July 1963.

Another reason frequently given for the alleged decline in the quality of councillors is the dominance of party politics in the administration of local affairs. When candidates are chosen by the parties, the unpolitical do not get much chance of public service: and even party stalwarts sometimes resent the excessive intrusion of politics into the conduct of council business. 'The council chamber is being reduced to a farce,' Aneurin Bevan once complained. 'The caucus is getting more powerful than the electorate.' Party politics have often figured prominently in local government in the past – there is the example of Eatanswill in *Pickwick Papers* and, more seriously, that of Birmingham in the days of Joseph Chamberlain, or of the London County Council at its inception in 1888 – but in recent years the power of the caucus has grown and party warfare has become more general.[1]

Local authorities are today much under discussion: Local Government Commissions have been carrying out surveys and Royal Commissions with wide terms of reference are considering their future. Their critics are numerous – this is a questioning age – but no reasonable person would deny that they play an important role in modern society. 'We believe,' Sir Winston Churchill once said, 'that the devolution of power and duties, and the building up of strong and well-equipped local authorities to exercise them, has still the dominant part to play in our modern domestic progress.' And it is interesting to note that distinguished civil servants, pre-eminent in central government, are among those most convinced of the need for strong local authorities as a counter-weight to centralized power. Many would rank John Anderson (Lord Waverley) as the wisest civil servant of our time, and he was always a staunch advocate of local authorities as bulwarks of freedom. 'It remains as true today as ever it was,' he maintained, 'that local self-government is the cradle of democracy, and those who undertake the task of creating machinery appropriate to the discharge of new public responsibilities will neglect this aspect at their peril.'[2]

In her role as candid friend, Dame Evelyn Sharp usually tempers her criticism with a whole-hearted affirmation of faith in

1. See G. Block, *Party Politics in Local Government*, Conservative Political Centre, 1962.   2. *British Government since 1918*, Foreword.

effective local government. 'Local authorities *have* suffered some diminution of their independence of action,' she observes:

Genuine efforts have been made by central government in recent years to check the trend; and to get rid of unnecessary controls. But we cannot escape the fact that central and local government are now locked in a tighter partnership than ever before and they must learn to accommodate themselves to this. But I don't think this means that we have to resign ourselves to a diminution of local government. The increasing power of central government means, surely, that it is more than ever important to foster an effective and independently minded system of local government; to provide a counterpoise.[1]

The Department of Education in its annual reports shows that it recognizes the value of the continuing partnership: and – while there may be differences about how to do it – there can be few, if any, in the education service who do not attach the utmost importance to distribution of power as a means of protecting freedom.[2] 'Because it wields such influence for good or ill, power in education,' declared Sir Ronald Gould, General Secretary of the National Union of Teachers, 'should be shared. It is too potent a weapon to be put into the hands of the Government alone.'[3]

How central and local governments should share responsibilities is a difficult and delicate question, but in 1949 the Government set up a committee and confronted it with this very question. The Local Government Manpower Committee, as well as advising about economy in the use of staff, was asked 'to examine in particular the distribution of function between central and local government.' In one of its reports it indicated six aspects of administration – six 'musts' – over which the Minister should exercise control; and, as he accepted the report, they constitute an official clue to the bewildering problem of who is responsible for what.[4] The Minister must, said the Committee:

1. *Public Administration*, 1962, Vol. 40, pp. 378–9. Article on 'The Future of Local Government'.
2. See Sir William Alexander, *Education in England*, p. 3.
3. N.U.T. Annual Conference, 1962.
4. See *Education in 1949*, H.M.S.O., 1950, pp. 1 and 2. The Minister of Education at the time was George Tomlinson who, like other good parliamentarians, had had long and important service on a local education authority.

1. Be satisfied that educational facilities and auxiliary services are provided in sufficient quantity and variety.
2. Be satisfied that educational establishments and auxiliary services are well managed, equipped, staffed, and maintained.
3. Ensure the proper freedom of parents, teachers, and other third parties.
4. Be satisfied of the qualification of teachers and medical officers to the extent necessary to safeguard their and the children's interests.
5. Control the fees charged and awards and allowances made to the extent necessary to safeguard the interests of local education, and other school authorities, parents and students.
6. Control the provision of educational premises.

The emphasis in these recommendations about the Minister's functions is, as it should be, on control with the implication that 'execution' is the local education authority's business. The Department of Education and Science does not provide or maintain schools or colleges or employ, pay or dismiss teachers; these functions are usually the responsibility of the local education authorities.[1] These authorities have a fine record of positive achievement from 1902 onwards, and there has certainly been no decline of purpose in recent years. Of that the 7,000 and more schools provided in the last twenty years are strong circumstantial evidence; consider the time, thought, and knowledge given to siting, planning, constructing, and equipping them.

There are some, however, who would prefer to see education 'go it alone', administered locally or regionally by an *ad hoc* body, that is to say by a board which, like the school boards created in 1870, would be concerned only with education. They point to the example of the Regional Hospital Boards, and think that a similarly constituted body might be suitable for the local government of education. There is much to be said, however, against the fragmentation of local government and the proliferation of separate boards for various services. It is, also, most unlikely that education would gain by being isolated nearly as much as it would lose. To give one example, in areas where land is scarce, as it often is, even

1. In 1970 the Secretary of State (Mr E. Short) opened the 10,000th school built since the war by L.E.A.s or voluntary bodies.

on new housing estates, how much less chance education would have of acquiring its fair share of suitable sites if it was out of touch with County or Town Hall.

It would, too, be bad for society as a whole, if the influence of education was removed from the Council Chamber. Close co-operation between public services is essential to a decent community life: and there must be some degree of coordination. The best kind of coordination is not the artificial brand bred in conferences and joint committees but the kind that comes naturally when members of a team meet frequently and informally. When he was Director of Education for Liverpool, Mr H. S. Magnay gave an interesting account of cooperation among different services there and, as one of several examples of such cooperation, showed how in that city 'the fact that all the chief and subordinate officers are officers of a single council is an important factor making for coordination'. 'It is natural,' he wrote, 'that a spirit of comradeship and partnership should develop among them, and that they should make use of the opportunity for meeting, thrown in their way, to discuss and coordinate policies.'[1]

LOOKING FORWARD

Education is now much the biggest item in the annual expenditure incurred by county and county borough councils. It accounts today for about 56 per cent of their budget, and the cost of the education service is bound to increase. They are, as noted earlier, spending about £1,500 million on it today, and the figure will almost certainly continue to increase. This should compel revision of the system of local finance and will probably lead to an increase in the government's share of the cost. But the changes in the local government of education are not likely to be restricted to finance. For although since 1944 there has been a growing realization of the importance of education, there has been little alteration, if any, in the way in which it is administered locally.

It is true that the 1944 Act effected some significant modifications in the administrative machinery: Part III authorities were abolished, and Excepted Districts and Divisional Executives were

1. Article, 'Liverpool: a Case Study in Coordination' in *The Annals*, The American Academy of Political and Social Sciences, 1955, Vol. 302.

created. But apart from this there has been no great change in the government of education in the counties, while in the county boroughs education is governed today much as it was under the Education Act of 1902. This may with some justification be reckoned a tribute to the wisdom of Balfour and Morant: but it may also, like the rates problem, be ascribed in part to delay in adjusting the local government of education to the circumstances of our time.

What, the cynic may ask, are these new circumstances? There are certainly some that should be somehow reflected in the local government of education. One is the big change that has taken place in the public esteem of teachers and in our attitude to expert opinion since 1902. The Education Act of 1902 (Section 17 (3)) required the appointment by the county or county borough council of an education committee on which, as well as a majority of aldermen and councillors, there had to be some coopted members with experience in education and knowledge of schools. There is a similar requirement in the 1944 Act (First Schedule, Part II) and, in selecting the coopted members, it is customary to include two or three representative teachers usually from among those teaching in the authority's area.[1] Except for a proviso in regard to the Agreed Syllabus for religious education this is the only statutory provision that creates an opportunity of associating teachers with the local government of education. The committee can, of course, if it wishes set up advisory committees and appoint teachers to serve on them: but that, though an admirable practice, is not part of the statutory pattern. Contrast this with the great importance attached to the Senate or to Academic Boards in university statutes and rules. It may be that the time has come when there should be a statutory teacher body in schemes for the local government of education, charged with the duty of considering aspects of administration that affect the inner life of school or college.

Another 'new circumstance' is the growing number of keen and enlightened parents; and yet another is the significance of the local community in modern society and the close relationship that

---

1. The requirement of the 1944 Act is: 'Every education committee of a local education authority shall include persons of experience in education and persons acquainted with the educational conditions prevailing in the area. . . .'

often exists informally between neighbourhood and school. Both of these 'circumstances' seem to deserve, if not demand, some official recognition: and this is already sometimes achieved by including representative parents and local leaders on governing and managerial bodies. But there could be more representation of this kind, and undoubtedly much more could be made of governing bodies. They could be accorded more status, and given more responsibility; and, in selecting their members, the criterion, now often political, could be ability to render useful and intelligent service to a particular school.

When the 1944 Act was in the throes of its Committee stage emphasis was laid on the value of governing bodies and, in response to requests made in Parliament, the Government issued a paper (Cmd 6523) on *Principles of Government in Maintained Secondary Schools.* 'Every school,' it urged, 'of whatever type or category must have an individual life of its own as well as a place in the local system. The fact that aided schools are assured under the Bill of an independence hardly, if at all, less than that which they enjoy at present, makes it the more desirable to seek means to secure that reasonable autonomy is enjoyed also by county, controlled, and special agreement schools. Independence implies, not freedom from proper control, but freedom to exercise legitimate and appropriate functions.' The paper then proceeded to enunciate principles under such headings as finance, appointment of teachers, internal organization, admission of pupils: but on the vital question of choosing the right sort of governors it had nothing to say. That is an aspect that now needs to be looked at critically.

No one has written more wisely than Lady Wootton about the importance of some of the lesser bodies in our administrative system. Stressing their value as 'safeguards of freedom' she observes so truly:

On this account the contribution and methods of appointment of these often apparently humble bodies deserve much attention. As things are, there is some tendency for them to draw upon too narrow a circle of membership. The easiest method of recruitment is to look to the political parties for nominations; but in this way the field of selection may be unwisely narrowed.[1]

1. *Freedom under Planning,* Allen and Unwin, 1945, p. 153.

Today there is usually no lack of good potential governors and managers, but they have to be sought and, sometimes, persuaded.

There is also the baffling problem of the size of area most suitable for the local government of education, and this is complicated by the fact that for some purposes a fairly small area is desirable, while for others, like technical education or the education of handicapped children, an area of considerable size is almost essential. But such issues have been considered over and over again by the Local Government Commissions: and, as a result of their deliberations, we shall no doubt see many changes in the structure of local government in the next few years.

It is interesting to note that those who now discuss the future of the local administration of education tend to dwell upon similar problems. For example, Professor Vaizey in his stimulating chapter on administration in his *Education for Tomorrow* considers among other problems the place of teachers and parents in the administrative system; regional authorities; finance; and school groups. Professor Gittins, with unique experience as a former Director of Education, Local Government Commissioner, and Professor of Education, has also looked forward, speculating tentatively about the future of L.E.A.s. 'Certain questions,' he writes, 'seem to be emerging which are likely to have a significant influence upon them.' Size, he sees as an obvious problem: and remarks upon 'the considerable demands which further education makes upon resources of capital and specialist manpower'. 'Is the small L.E.A. therefore doomed?' he asks. Another of his questions is: 'Will the teachers' organizations play a fuller part in policy making?' 'Nothing,' he replies, 'would do more to make teaching a nobler profession than that L.E.A.s should trust them, and should be seen to trust them, to do a professional job.' 'Education is in politics,' he remarks, 'and will never be separated from it. Even so it is relevant to ask . . . do politicians presume too far in exercising authority over schools and colleges?' 'And what of parents?' he concludes, '. . . Something more than parent-teacher associations is called for, admirable as these are. In an ideal system the voice of parents would be heard at the school governors' table and in the education committee itself.'[1]

1. Article on 'The L.E.A.: Retrospect and Prospect' in *Education*, Vol. 121, pp. 31, 32, 4 January 1963.

COMMITTEES

Whatever form the government of education may take in the future, we can be fairly certain that committees and sub-committees will be a prominent feature in its operation, both nationally and locally and maybe at the regional level also. For, largely because we believe in government by discussion, we make a habit of setting up official committees, and among our public-spirited fellow-citizens there are not a few who seem to welcome opportunities to serve on them. These official committees are of several kinds: advisory, negotiating, legislative, scrutinizing, and administrative.[1] The education service can provide many examples of the advisory type: e.g. the Central Advisory Councils on Education prescribed in the 1944 Education Act for England and for Wales and in the Education (Scotland) Act, 1945, for Scotland; the Schools Council for the Curriculum and Examinations; the National Advisory Council on the Training and Supply of Teachers; and the National Advisory Council for Industry and Commerce. There are also the Regional Councils for Further Education which give advice about coordination and development; and many local education authorities have their own advisory councils appointed for various purposes.

Often these councils and committees fulfil more than one function: and, indeed, it is usual for an Advisory Council to do a great deal of 'inquiring' before formulating its 'advice'. Both the Crowther and Robbins Committees are examples of this: for they buttress their recommendations with information based on surveys and researches carried out on their behalf and published, in part, as supplements to their reports. The Fleming Committee on The Public School and the Educational System is an interesting case of a committee that 'inquired' more effectively than it 'advised': its picture of the past is much more convincing than are its proposals for the future. The Burnham Committee with its panels of local authorities and teachers is a good example of a negotiating committee even though, after forty years, it suffered

1. See K. C. Wheare's *Government by Committee*, Oxford University Press, 1955: a book that is already a classic.

an eclipse and has run into much stormy weather.[1] Other negotiating committees deal with the salaries of teachers in farm institutes, the salaries of teaching staff in training colleges, and the salaries of inspectors and organizers in the service of local education authorities.

For examples of legislative committees one must look to Parliament. There Education Bills have to run the gauntlet of the procedure observed in the House of Commons for such legislation – the First and Second Readings, the Committee Stage, Report and Third Reading. In addition to legislation of a national character there can be local Bills promoted by individual local authorities wishing to obtain powers beyond those provided by national legislation. Such 'local Bills' are considered by a Committee of the Houses of Parliament, before which the promoting authority and other interested parties have the right to appear and be represented by counsel. By this procedure enterprising local authorities have from time to time been able to take a forward step in education or improve the social environment in ways not yet adopted by the country as a whole.

Parliament also provides two good examples of committees that 'scrutinize', namely the Committee of Public Accounts and the Committee on Estimates: their purpose is to check extravagance and promote efficiency. Local authorities, also – especially in times of financial stress – set up committees to examine expenditure critically, and their finance committees, more particularly when annual estimates are under review, can be assiduous in their search for economies. Of committees that administer there is no better example than the education committee in a county or county borough. County and county borough councils are required by law to appoint an education committee and it is the instrument whereby they, as local education authorities, administer education for their area. It reports to the council monthly, though in some areas less frequently; and usually it has something like thirty or forty members, of whom the coopted amount to about one third. Among the latter, as already mentioned, there are usually two or three teachers and, normally, there are

1. See Remuneration of Teachers Act, 1963 and 1965, and *The Burnham Story*, Councils and Education Press, 1963.

about three representatives of the churches: for example, an Anglican, a Roman Catholic, and a representative of the Free Churches. It is customary, also, to have a university representative.

The education committee does its work through a number of main sub-committees, some of which – owing to the volume of work – also delegate business to smaller sub-committees. In the city of Nottingham – to give one example – there are seven main sub-committees which are respectively responsible for the administration of primary education, secondary education, further education, special services, sites and buildings, youth employment, and finance and general purposes. Every local education authority is required to appoint a Chief Education Officer and the appointment has to be approved by the Minister. He is supported by a professional and clerical staff, including a local inspectorate: and among the principal officers there are generally assistant education officers for such branches of the service as primary, secondary, and further education.

The local administration of education is very different from the relatively detached and remote control exercised by the Minister and his civil servants.[1] What makes it fascinating is that it is a very human business, and those responsible are – or should be – in close touch with their problems and operate with a first-hand knowledge of the persons concerned, the places, the buildings, and the local conditions. Sir Graham Balfour, one of the great local administrators of the 1902 Education Act gave two lectures – famous in their day – at Birmingham University in which he tried to convey to his audience the nature of his task as Director of Education for Staffordshire. Just before closing, he said:

I must have made my points very badly if it has not yet been realized that I regard the Personal Element as the essence of local administration. No two persons and no two places are alike in this world in my experience, and if you do not know enough of local circumstances or local personalities to take them in to account in your administration you are likely to be a Bureaucrat.[2]

1. For a sympathetic account of the civil-servant tradition see Lord Bridges' Rede Lecture, *Portrait of a Profession*, Cambridge University Press, 1950.
2. *Educational Administration*, Oxford University Press, 1921, p. 51.

Some Thoughts about Administration

Much depends upon the quality of the chairman of the education committee, and this was never more true than it is today when education is such a prominent service. At one time it was usual to select as chairman someone thought to be particularly suitable to act as leader and spokesman in the local administration of education: and, having appointed him, to regard the decision as a life sentence. If the choice was a good one, this practice of retaining the same chairman indefinitely had advantages. The chairman got to know the educational problems of the area, was himself well known in the schools, and often became a public figure able to advance the cause of education nationally as well as in his local arena. His long tenure of the chair also helped to ensure continuity in local policy, often a valuable asset because it enables schools to develop with a sense of security.

But, on the other hand, there is much to be said against the practice of having a long-term chairman. A non-stop occupation of the chair has its dangers, and not least the temptation to become arbitrary and autocratic; and a very real weakness of such a practice is that it deprives other members of the committee of the opportunities and experience that a period in the chair provides. It is, largely for such reasons, now unusual to let chairmen continue in office for an indefinite time. Politics have also become an important factor in determining the choice of chairmen and ways of choosing him. The long-term chairman has become a rarity, and committees today are inclined to go to the opposite extreme and make the tenure of the chair too short. If, as often happens, there is an understanding that chairmen of the main sub-committees shall serve for the same period as the chairman of the education committee, this practice of changing chairmen frequently can become an unsettling influence. Professor Wheare favours 'a time-limit of something like five years', and that seems a reasonable period.[1]

THE PROFESSIONALS

Our system of government is largely based, as Bagehot noted, on 'a due mixture of special and non-special minds' or, as a

1. *Government by Committee*, p. 180.

contemporary described it, on 'an odd combination of amateur and professional administrators, the amateurs controlling the professionals'.[1] As we have already noted, at the centre the Minister is assisted by his Department of civil servants. In the counties and county boroughs the education committee, the governors and the managers provide the non-special or amateur element, while the Chief Education Officer and the staff in the local education office are the professionals. There is often a close and happy working partnership between the chairman of the education committee and the Chief Education Officer, and this can prove very helpful in promoting smooth administration and speeding developments.

From their first days after the passing of the 1902 Act, local education authorities have attached great importance to teaching experience when appointing education officers, and with rare exceptions they have been recruited from the teaching profession. The educational renaissance, now in ferment, makes a strong school background more than ever an essential qualification. But we live in a managerial society, and there are those who maintain that administration is, *sui generis*, a special skill that enables those who have acquired it to apply it effectively in various branches of industry or in different governmental services. Lord Russell drew attention to the growing influence of this doctrine as far back as 1932, observing: 'It thus happens, as organizations increase in size, that the important positions of power tend, more and more, to be in the hands of men who have no intimate familiarity with the purposes of the work that they organize.'[2]

While local authorities have always attached importance to administrative ability when choosing senior officers for their different services they normally act on the principle that their services should be managed by officers with the appropriate professional background. They take this line not because they do not believe in training for management but on certain practical grounds. Their point of view was admirably expounded by Sir Harold Banwell in a discussion about the education of administra-

1. Bagehot, *The English Constitution*, Kegan Paul, 1909 ed., p. 197. Sir Ivor Jennings, *The Queen's Government*, Penguin Books, 1954, p. 104.

2. *Education and the Social Order*, Allen and Unwin, first published 1932, 1951 ed., p. 240.

tors in which Lord Bridges, Colonel Urwick, Mr D. K. Clarke of the Administrative Staff College, Henley, and others participated. 'You will observe,' he said, 'that most administrators in local government have one thing in common: they are members of a profession.' They are, he explained, lawyers, accountants, doctors of medicine, architects, or, in the case of the education officers, they have been teachers. 'In local government,' he continued, 'professional qualifications are insisted upon because of the nature of the tasks to be performed: but it is true to say that these qualifications could not have been obtained without a good educational background. Specialized professional knowledge has been the essential requirement: but, in the result, officers have been secured who have much the same outlook as those who enter the administrative class of the civil service.'[1]

It is for such reasons that local education authorities, when appointing their chief or assistant education officers, usually ask for a good degree, teaching experience, and experience in educational administration. This typically British emphasis on experience should not, of course, be interpreted as implying that weight is not also attached to other factors, including appropriate postgraduate study at a university or staff college.[2] A serious weakness in the establishment structure of local government services and, indeed, in that of the civil service and other fields of employment, is the almost unbridgable gulf between the highest and other grades. There have always been men and women of high ability in the middle reaches of the service who have been barred by lack of educational opportunity in their youth from obtaining the university or other qualifications deemed necessary for the senior positions.

Much has been done in recent years, by means of training schemes and in other ways, to minimize the injustice of the situation: and in the education departments of local authorities a few members of the administrative staff have availed themselves of

1. *The Making of an Administrator*, edited by A. Dunsire, Manchester University Press, 1956, pp. 60–71.
2. For American views on this question, see John Walton, *Administration and Policy Making in Education*, Johns Hopkins Press, Baltimore, 1959, especially Chapter 2.

opportunities to qualify as teachers and so gain the teaching experience so often required for senior posts. The development of secondary education for all has begun to reduce the size of the injustice but, for a solution of the problem, much depends upon the speedy fulfilment of the Robbins Committee's axiom that 'courses of higher education should be available for all those who are qualified by ability and attainment to pursue them, and who wish to do so'.[1]

WILLING TO SERVE

It is characteristic of committees that they grow and multiply; 'we are overrun by them,' as Sir Winston Churchill once said, 'like the Australians were by the rabbits.' Professor Wheare calculates 'that the grand total of committees in local government is round about 50,000'.[2] In the academic world they, also, proliferate and consume valuable hours that could be devoted to teaching or research: so considerable are their demands that some of our scientists have given this as a reason for their flight to the U.S.A. We owe much to those who, often at great personal inconvenience, serve on exacting committees. It is not always realized how much time and energy important committees absorb. The Robbins Committee provides a good example of devoted service: to produce this report the distinguished team of eleven busy persons scorned delights and lived laborious days for almost two and a half years. They held 111 meetings, visited many universities and colleges, held innumerable interviews, paid short visits to France, the Federal German Republic, the Netherlands, Sweden, and Switzerland, and longer visits to the United States and the Soviet Union.

While it is generally realized that we owe some of our greatest educational reforms to the work of Advisory Committees, it is sometimes forgotten that from 1902 onwards local education authorities – in addition to their administrative duties – have played an important missionary role, often championing causes that would have made little progress if they had not backed them strongly. Sometimes they have fought their battles separately, and

1. Vol. I, p. 8.   2. *Government by Committee*, p. 166.

pioneered in particular fields: e.g. Bradford in school health and nursery schools, London and Manchester in central schools, Cambridgeshire in village colleges, and Anglesey in rural comprehensive schools. And sometimes the battle has been fought collectively through the local authority associations – the Association of Municipal Corporations, the County Councils Association, the Welsh Joint Education Committee, and the Association of Education Committees. The Association of Education Committees in conference, pursuing in full cry some urgent reform, can be a dramatic occasion. There have been conferences when by their humanity and conviction speakers – often men and women who have come up the hard way – have so stirred the public conscience that notable advances have become accepted policy. How often over the years has the A.E.C. pressed again and again for the raising of the school leaving age and helped it on its uphill journey from thirteen to sixteen.

Happily all such conferences and committees have their human side, and anyone interested in the lighter side of committee life will enjoy F. M. Cornford's *Microsmographia Academica*, a gentle satire on committee habits in the University of Cambridge.[1] The types that he pillories are, however, not confined to the academic world but are to be found in all committee rooms: for example, who does not know the *non-placet* for whom the time is never opportune, who always fears 'the thin end of the wedge', and deplores 'the dangerous precedent'; or 'the bore' who talks slowly and indistinctly at a little distance from the point? As E. V. Lucas once said, 'Committees may all be different but they are very largely the same. The members are types.' And he too describes many of them: e.g. the habitual late-comer who enters stealthily and tip-toes to his chair; the member who must get all his salutations made before he settles down; and the member who begins 'with all due deference, Mr Chairman'.[2] While committees like their formalities, their ritual, their minutes, and their formidable agenda, they are a very human institution and life would be very bureaucratic without them.

---

1. Bowes and Bowes, 4th ed., 1949.
2. Essay on 'Committees' in *Selected Modern Essays: Second Series*, Oxford University Press (World's Classics), 1932.

CHAPTER 7

The Changing Pattern of Higher Education

THE DAWN OF A NEW ERA

REVOLUTIONS, it has often been said, do not happen suddenly: they are usually the outcome of forces that have been at work long before it becomes obvious that big changes are imminent. Something of this kind has been taking place in the normally tranquil realm of higher education; and gradually we have reached a situation which will almost certainly bring 'change, wide and deep' and profoundly alter the pattern of higher education as we know it today. Of the many influences that have combined to produce this revolutionary climate none has been more powerful than the growing popular demand for more and better higher education. This is largely the result of developments in secondary education in recent years and the increasing tendency to stay longer at school. Most boys and girls in sixth and similar senior forms want to continue their education after leaving school, and there has been a steadily rising demand for places in universities and colleges. 'Recent years have seen a massive expansion of numbers in higher education, an expansion which has been accelerated by the adoption of the principle that virtually all United Kingdom residents admitted to undergraduate, or similar, courses in higher education are automatically entitled to financial support. The number of students in receipt of awards ... has almost doubled over the last five years, and the cost has much more than doubled.'[1]

But this demand for more and better higher education has come not only from prospective students, backed by eager parents, but in recent years even more strongly from statesmen and others concerned about the future of the nation. 'The growing realization of this country's economic dependence upon the education of its population,' said the Robbins Committee, 'has led to much questioning of the adequacy of present arrangements. Unless

1. *Education Statistics for the United Kingdom*, H.M.S.O., 1970, p. xiii.

higher education is speedily reformed, it is argued, there is little hope of this densely populated island maintaining an adequate position in the fiercely competitive world of the future.'[1] As far back as 1945 the Percy Committee on Higher Technological Education stressed the need and showed the way for advance in that vital field, but for more than a decade progress was prevented by a prolonged and somewhat discreditable controversy. The main issue of this time-consuming conflict was whether the nation should look to universities or to technical colleges for the technologists so sorely needed. Eventually, however, the massive developments in higher education in the U.S.A., Russia, and Western Europe led to action. The controversy was halted, the Government coming to the obvious conclusion that we desperately needed all the scientists and technologists that our universities and colleges of technology together could provide. 'Each,' the Government at last decided, 'has its own distinctive contribution to make to the development of technological education, and the aim is to expand facilities at both.'[2]

The persistent demand for higher education is also largely due to the social revolution of our time – the increasing prosperity, the wider distribution of income, and the desire to advance in the social scale. 'Educational qualifications are, as Weber emphasized, a substitute for birth or ascriptive claims to a style of life.'[3] Another reason for the demand is the importance attached in modern society to examinations and to their use as a criterion for admission into ruling and managerial élites. And as the élites grow in size, so does the demand for higher education. 'A society like ours today needs a far larger élite,' writes Sir Edward Boyle, ' – in science, commerce, administration, and the professions.'[4] Scientific industrialism, especially, makes an ever increasing demand for well-educated staff and enhances the importance of research in universities and colleges of technology. Dr Halsey has

1. Vol. I, p. 5.
2. White Paper on *Technical Education*, Cmd 9703, H.M.S.O., 1956, p. 12.
3. Article by A. H. Halsey on 'British Universities', *Archives Européennes de Sociologie*, Vol. III, no. I, 1962, p. 90.
4. *Universities Quarterly*, March 1962, p. 129.

aptly summarized the complex situation that confronts universities today:

The Biritish universities in company with such institutions all over the industrialized and industrializing world are in an agony of adaptation to pressures towards expansion. In the short run expansive pressure springs from the post-war birth-rate bulge, in the not so short run from rising popular aspirations towards higher education and in the long run (i.e. fundamentally) from the economic implications of a culture which is based increasingly on science.[1]

As the following figures given in the Robbins Report[2] show, the number of students engaged full-time in higher education in Great Britain increased greatly during the post-war period:

	University	Teacher Training	Further Education	Total
1938–9	50,000	13,000	6,000	69,000
1954–5	82,000	28,000	12,000	122,000
1962–3	118,000	55,000	43,000	216,000

While much has been done in recent years to provide suitable teaching staff and accommodation for these additional numbers it has been difficult, if not impossible, to pursue a planned, coherent, policy. For higher education in this country has evolved under various auspices in response to need, and its institutions have their different traditions and forms of government. There is much to be said for such diversity, and in the *laissez-faire* world of the last century it was appropriate that institutions should go their separate ways, but an unqualified separatism does not harmonize with the planned economy of today.

With expansion continuing on several fronts it became more and more obvious that a comprehensive survey of higher education was urgently necessary: it is folly to expand in this direction and that without more knowledge of what is needed and of how best to provide it. Higher education was a mighty maze without a plan, and we had speedily to create a system based on well-considered aims and principles. And there were kindred problems

1. op. cit., p. 86.
2. Vol. I, p. 15.

urgently requiring attention. One of the more difficult was the relationship between the state and the universities now that the latter have become largely dependent on public funds. In 1938–9 the Treasury's contribution to their cost was no more than 35·8 per cent: by 1953–4 the percentage had risen to 70·5: and it is now moving towards 75. And yet another issue awaiting settlement was the status of some institutions, other than universities, in which important developments had taken place. We now had colleges of technology doing work at degree level while the training colleges, their course lengthened to three years, were attaining standards of university quality. And there are great institutions in London, Glasgow, and Manchester doing outstanding work in technological education and research.

It was for such reasons that the Government appointed the Robbins Committee with as its terms of reference:

To review the pattern of full-time higher education in Great Britain and in the light of national needs and resources to advise Her Majesty's Government on what principles its long-term development should be based. In particular, to advise in the light of these principles, whether there should be any changes in that pattern, whether any new types of institution are desirable and whether any modifications shall be made in the present arrangements for planning and coordinating the development of the various types of institution.

The Committee reported in October 1963, and among its many wise observations about higher education there was none more appropriate than the comment: 'We are now passing into a new era.'

WHAT IS 'HIGHER EDUCATION'?

'Let us not be in a hurry to define,' Lord Baldwin once wisely observed. 'Definitions and the desire for definitions split Christendom into fragments in its early days, and it has not recovered yet.' There are several other good reasons for not defining, and among them the very practical one that it is an occupation that consumes precious time. But, alas, there are occasions when a definition is essential and the Robbins Committee rightly took trouble to define the meaning that they attached to the words 'higher education' as used in their terms of reference. It is all the more important to be clear about this new interpretation because for over forty years (1902–44) 'higher education' carried the meaning assigned to it in the 1902 Education Act, namely education that was not elementary.

In the Robbins Report it bears a very different meaning; and as, doubtless, in future years 'higher education' will figure prominently in our educational discussions with this new connotation it is well to be clear about it. The Committee devoted a page of their report to the defining process, and one cannot here reproduce it in full. But it is important to give this new official interpretation of 'higher education' in the Committee's own words, and the following extract, while not comprehensive, gives the pith of the definition:

In the main we have concentrated on the universities in Great Britain and those colleges, within the purview of the Ministry of Education and the Scottish Education Department, that provide courses for the education and training of teachers or systematic courses of further education beyond the Advanced Level of the General Certificate of Education or beyond the Ordinary National Certificate or its equivalent. In further education the above definition embraces, in addition to the Colleges of Technology, the advanced work undertaken at a great number of technical and commercial colleges and schools of art; but it excludes the initial stages of much professional and other education provided in such colleges. We have something to say about the Agricultural Colleges and about full-time courses of adult education, since at certain points their development is related to our central theme.[1]

Having noted this 'definition' let us now consider briefly some of the problems of government that particularly affect the three institutions named – universities, training colleges, colleges of advanced technology.[2]

HOW UNIVERSITIES ARE GOVERNED

Facts and figures about education today soon get out of date, and

1. Vol. I, p. 2.
2. For an up-to-date survey see Mountford, *British Universities*, O.U.P., 1966.

it may well be that those given in this chapter will not be valid for long. But, subject to that reservation, we can say that in Great Britain there are now over forty universities. Reference has already been made to the older ones. Until the second quarter of the nineteenth century there were only six: England had its two medieval foundations at Oxford and Cambridge, while Scotland had four dating from the fifteenth and sixteenth centuries. In the eighteen-thirties Durham was established and so was London, now a mighty federation of colleges, schools, and institutions. Later in the nineteenth century came the older civic universities, of which Manchester is the largest with about 9,000 students, including those studying technology at the College of Science and Technology.

The University of Wales is, like London, a federation of colleges, the earliest (Aberystwyth) having been founded in 1872. Next in date came the younger civic universities of which six were established as university colleges in the years before and after the First World War: and they were later accorded university status. Keele, founded after the Second World War, became a university in 1962. Then there is the group of seven recent foundations, located at Brighton, Norwich, York, Canterbury, Colchester, Coventry, and Lancaster. For them there was no novitiate as a university college: they were created universities from the start with full degree-giving powers.

A university is a legal corporation with certain privileges and powers: 'first and foremost – the hall-mark and crucial differentia of a university is the right to confer degrees.'[1] During the Middle Ages, as we noted earlier, there were various centres of learning, but law and custom prescribed that only those authorized by papal or imperial decree should rank as universities and have the right to award degrees. In later times, when Christendom had divided, other ways of conferring university status were adopted, and in this country most of our universities derive their powers from a Royal Charter or an Order in Council.[2] But no less important than this legal conferment of privileges and powers is the

1. Grant Robertson, *British Universities*, Benn, 1930, p. 18.
2. But for a good legal exposition of how universities obtain their powers see Robbins Report, Vol. IV, Section I.

strong tradition of self-government that has come down from the past. 'The medieval creators,' it has been well said, 'bequeathed to the modern world the sovereign lesson that the organization of higher education must be delegated as a responsible trust to those who are prepared to devote their lives to learning its secrets, maintaining its standards, and perpetually training their successors in the discharge of these duties.'[1]

Our universities attach great importance to this right to manage their own affairs: and they have been careful to safeguard it both in their relations with the state and in their domestic policy. When they began to receive aid from the exchequer on a substantial scale, there were fears that their traditional liberties might be encroached upon. There was a particularly critical phase after the First World War. Costs had increased and there was urgent need for development and expansion: increased grants were essential, but could they be obtained without conceding some measure of state control? Fortunately Herbert Fisher was then President of the Board of Education and, as a distinguished Oxford tutor for many years and more recently Vice-Chancellor of Sheffield University, he fully appreciated the implications of the problem.

And there was another helpful coincidence. To quote Fisher's own words: 'Austen Chamberlain was fortunately Chancellor of the Exchequer. He was himself an alumnus of Cambridge, and the son of the founder of Birmingham University.'[2] They agreed that the best way of finding a good solution was a Royal Commission, and they persuaded Lord Oxford (H. H. Asquith), the great Liberal statesman and a devoted son of Balliol, to be its chairman. As a result of the Commission's report the University Grants Committee was established as the channel of government grant. Ever since, this Committee, acting under the Treasury and composed mainly of persons with an academic background, has distributed the grant to the general satisfaction of the Treasury and the universities. But as a result of the mounting expenditure on universities it has since 1968 been a condition of grant that the books and records of the U.G.C., concerning grant,

1. Grant Robertson, op. cit., p. 9.
2. *Unfinished Autobiography*, pp. 115–16.

should be open to inspection by the Comptroller and Auditor General.

By means of the University Grants Committee it has been possible to have a national university policy without violating the freedom of each university to order its own affairs. Universities attach great importance to this freedom not only in their relations with the state but also in the conduct of their domestic policy. The organization of their internal government is that of a self-governing community. Oxford and Cambridge established that tradition although, because of their collegiate system, they have their distinctive constitutions. Their colleges are independent societies which, subject to statutes, are autonomous. Responsibility for university policy and practice rests in these two older universities with bodies elected or appointed by members of the university. Lay or non-academic persons have no share in their government, but in Scottish universities the Court, a small body of predominantly lay membership, is the supreme governing and executive body.

In England and Wales all the universities except Oxford and Cambridge, are governed internally under a dual system. All academic business is dealt with by the Senate and its committees: and the Senate is a wholly academic body, composed entirely of professors and other members of the teaching staff. Non-academical business, on the other hand, especially finance and external relations, is normally dealt with by the Council, an executive governing body, usually small and with a strong proportion of lay members, men and women eminent in the region in which the university is situated. There is, also, a Court, with a general supervisory function: and this, as a rule, is a large body consisting partly of academic members but mainly of representatives of county, county borough, and other councils in the university's neighbourhood.

The predominance of lay representatives on Court and Council has its critics in academic circles, and apparently submissions on this theme were made to the Robbins Committee. But they were not impressed. 'We are,' they state, 'not in sympathy with this view. More than 85 per cent of university finance comes from public sources and in our judgement it is in general neither practical or justifiable that the spending of university funds should be wholly in the hands of the users. Academic autonomy is more likely to be safeguarded where the public has a guarantee that there is independent lay advice and criticism within the universities.'[1]

The Vice-Chancellor or Principal is an important figure in university government. He is at the centre, often as chairman, of the various discussions affecting internal policy or relations with the outside world. He represents the university in many negotiations, including those with the University Grants Committee; and he is, of course, a member of that influential body, the Committee of Vice-Chancellors and Principals. 'The selection of a Vice-Chancellor or Principal is,' the Robbins Committee truly observed, 'perhaps the most important decision that the governing body of a university may be called upon to make.'[2]

COLLEGES OF EDUCATION

Throughout the post-war years the spotlight has been on our training colleges: they have been under pressure to educate more and more teachers. Until recently they were mostly small communities, nearly a hundred of them having less than 250 students. In recent years expansion has proceeded rapidly, many colleges being greatly enlarged and new ones established. There are now 164 in England and Wales, and it looks as if, with the U.E.D. students, the Robbins target of 111,000 by 1973-4 will be exceeded well before that date. But that will not satisfy the demand and the expansion must continue: it is estimated that by 1980 there will be approximately 130,000 students. In Scotland such institutions were more happily named: having long been called Colleges of Education. There are seven of them, two being much larger than any college south of the Border. They plan to increase the number of students from about 8,000 to over 11,000 by 1974.

The Minister of Education, being responsible for the staffing

1. Vol. I, pp. 217-18.
2. ibid., p. 221.

of all grant-aided schools in England and Wales, has the task of deciding how many teachers shall be trained and for what type of school. It is he who decides the number and size of colleges. On such crucial issues he is advised by the National Advisory Council on the Training and Supply of Teachers; and among questions on which this body has given advice have been the lengthening of the course of study in training colleges to three years, the present expansion of the colleges, and the need to adjust the balance of training as between the secondary and primary stage. There was general regret when in 1965 its deliberations were halted as a result of 'fundamental conflicts of interest about issues of national policy'.[1] There is a similar body in Scotland, the Scottish Council for the Training of Teachers.

The first training colleges were established in the nineteenth century by voluntary, mainly religious, bodies. Under the 1902 Act local authorities were also empowered to provide them, and they are responsible for about 100 of these colleges. So there is a kind of dual system, and there are different arrangements for the administration and finance of the two types of college. The voluntary colleges are direct grant institutions and receive a grant from the Ministry of Education that virtually covers their net recurrent expenditure. The Ministry also pays 75 per cent of the approved capital expenditure. Local authority colleges are financed under a pooling system to which all L.E.A.s contribute. In this way each college is the financial concern of L.E.A.s as a whole, and not of the local authority responsible for its administration. While students in training colleges are normally non-graduate there are in some a few graduates taking a one-year course. But most graduates who wish to obtain a professional qualification for teaching take a year's course in a university department of education. Such departments are governed and financed by their universities.

A great landmark in the history of teacher education in this country was the publication of the McNair Report in 1944. It has done much to raise the status and improve the quality of teacher training. One of its recommendations led to the introduction of the three-year (instead of two-year) course. Another brought

1. *Education in 1965*, H.M.S.O., 1966, p. 15.

about the establishment of Institutes of Education. There was a divergence of opinion in the McNair Committee on the subject of the best kind of regional organization for the training of teachers. One group wanted an entirely new form of organization that would associate the training colleges with the universities, while the other group sponsored a more modest proposal. Fortunately the first alternative proved the more acceptable and, with one exception, the universities decided to establish Institutes of Education with, as members, the university education department, the training colleges, and the art training centres attached to colleges or schools of art in the area.

Each Institute has a governing body or Council, the members of which include representatives nominated by the Senate, together with representatives of the member colleges and of the local authorities and teachers of the area. This Council is the supreme authority for teacher education in the region, subject only to the statutes of the university and the regulations of the Minister. But in all business that is not strictly administrative the Council is advised by an Academic Board, which itself sets up panels to report to it on various aspects of teacher education in the area.[1] The Institutes have done a great work in bringing together in different purposeful ways those concerned with teacher education in their regions, and they have fulfilled admirably the duties specifically assigned to them in the official regulations, namely 'to supervise and to secure the cooperation of establishments for the training of teachers within the area, to recommend students for acceptance by the Minister as qualified teachers, and to promote the study of education in the area'.

Impressed by the progress made by the training colleges in recent years and by the achievements of the Institutes of Education, the Robbins Committee made a number of recommendations designed to raise the status of teacher education. They proposed that: (1) the training colleges should, like their Scottish equivalents, be named Colleges of Education; (2) a college of education with less than 750 students should be an exception; (3) four-year courses leading to a degree (B.Ed.) and a professional

1. For a good detailed account of the work of Institutes of Education see Robbins Report, Vol. IV, pp. 46–9.

qualification should be provided in these colleges for suitable students; (4) the colleges belonging to each university's Institute of Education and the university education department should be formed into a School of Education; (5) on the academic side, each 'School' should be responsible to the university Senate for the degrees awarded to students in Colleges of Education; (6) L.E.A.s should be appropriately represented on the governing bodies both of the colleges for which they are at present responsible and of the Schools of Education; (7) the colleges should have independent governing bodies and should be financed by earmarked grants made by a Grants Commission (a new and larger replacement of the University Grants Committee) through universities to Schools of Education, and the Commission should have a Standing Committee for this purpose; (8) the voluntary colleges should be included in Schools of Education, subject to some modifications of the general financial arrangements; (9) the Scottish Colleges should be financed by grants from the Grants Commission.

The proposals were generally welcomed and those of a more academic character soon met with official approval. But the Government decided that it was inopportune to make changes in the financial and administrative character of the colleges 'at a time when they were engaged in a very large and rapid expansion, and when the problems of teacher supply were specially difficult'. In 1965, however, the Secretary of State appointed a Study Group to review the arrangements for the internal government of the colleges, and its report has led to helpful developments in their administration.[1] On the academic side much will depend on the sympathetic cooperation of the universities, and it has been good to note the arrangements that are being widely made for four-year courses leading to a B.Ed. degree. It has been well said that 'if the new policy is to work the Schools of Education will not only have to be accepted as a responsibility of the universities but accepted ungrudgingly and gladly'.[2]

1. *Report of the Study Group on the Government of Colleges of Education*, H.M.S.O., 1966.
2. Report of the Church of England Board of Education on *The Church and the Newsom and Robbins Reports*, p. 12.

THE GOVERNMENT OF TECHNICAL EDUCATION

In his valuable book, *Technical Education: its Aims, Organization, and Future Development*, Sir Peter Venables has a fine chapter about 'Freedom and Governance'.[1] It is, in effect, a cogent plea for much more freedom for technical colleges, and a firm declaration of faith in the merits of 'strong governing bodies'. Since 1955, when the book was first published, much consideration has been given to the government of technical education, and now under the Further Education (Local Education Authorities) Regulations of 1959 major establishments of further education (broadly all those with a good proportion of day students) are required to have governing bodies. Moreover in a departmental circular (7/59) the Minister gives local authorities much detailed advice about the functions that should be delegated to governors. The aim is to ensure that governors have a wide discretion in the administration of colleges of further education.

One of the most important developments in the organization of technical education in recent years has been the designation of ten major colleges as Colleges of Advanced Technology (C.A.T.s). Here, too, great attention has been paid to the method of government. At first the Government thought it best that these colleges in their new status should be administered by local education authorities but with the understanding that they would be accorded an independence 'appropriate to the academic level of their work'. 'There are those,' the Government maintained, 'who argue that a college of technology cannot be successfully administered within the framework of local government. The Government do not accept this. Local authorities take great pride in such colleges and often have been willing to find more money for them than the pressure on national resources has allowed them to spend.'[2]

The colleges did well. 'Seldom,' said the Ministry in a burst of enthusiasm, 'has so new a departure been so swiftly accomplished.'[3] But in spite of this the Government soon decided to

1. Published by Bell, 1955.
2. White Paper on *Technical Education*, Cmd 9703, H.M.S.O., 1956, p. 12.
3. *Education in 1962*, p. 7.

relieve local authorities of their responsibility; and in 1962 the C.A.T.s became direct-grant institutions with independent governing bodies representative of industry and commerce, professional and scientific institutions, local authorities, universities, and of their own academic boards. The Robbins Committee did not, however, think this measure of autonomy nearly adequate. 'We consider,' they wrote, 'that the present powers and status of the colleges are not commensurate with the work they are now doing. They lack many of the attributes of university self-government; they have not full power to award their own qualifications, and in particular cannot award degrees, despite the fact that their curricula, staffing, and facilities are adjudged by the National Council for Technological Awards to be appropriate for work for honours degrees.'[1] So they recommended that the colleges should become technological universities and that immediate steps be taken to grant charters.

The creation of the National Council for Technological Awards was partly due to the reluctance to accord technical colleges university status. It was established for the purpose of awarding Diplomas in Technology (Dip. Tech.), as an alternative to degrees, to approved students of honours degree quality in leading technical colleges. It was appreciated that they ought to have the opportunity of gaining, if not a degree, some equivalent award; and, as these students were not in a university, it was assumed that they could not be given a degree. 'For,' wrote Lord Percy in the important report that bears his name, 'the power to award degrees is the distinguishing mark of a university.'[2] This National Council did its work well and year after year was able to report that increasing numbers had sought its awards, which included in addition to the Dip. Tech. a higher degree roughly equivalent to a Ph.D.

But it seemed to many to be anomalous that Colleges of Advanced Technology should not have the power to grant their own degrees. The Robbins Committee were firmly of that opinion. 'Many of them,' they declared, referring to these colleges, 'have a long history and extensive academic experience.

1. Vol. I, p. 131.
2. *Higher Technological Education*, H.M.S.O., 1945.

While the universities founded in the last two or three years are allowed to award degrees from the beginning, subject only to the presence of an Academic Advisory Committee, these colleges are kept in a position of tutelage so that they are less attractive to students and their recruitment of staff is impeded.'[1]

The conferment of university status has not only ended this frustrating anomaly but also crowned the efforts of those who have striven for so long to secure for such colleges their rightful place in our modern society. As for the National Council for Technological Awards the Robbins Committee recommended that it should be replaced by a Council for National Academic Awards covering the whole of Great Britain, and that it should be empowered, perhaps by Royal Charter, to award honours and pass degrees to students in regional and area Colleges of Further Education and their Scottish equivalents.[2]

Impressed by some of the great technological institutions in countries that they visited – the Massachusetts Institute of Technology and the Technical High Schools at Zurich and Delft – the Robbins Committee recommended that there should be developed in Britain, as university institutions, a small number of 'Special Institutions for Scientific and Technological Education and Research'. They proposed that Imperial College in London, and the Colleges of Science and Technology in Manchester and Glasgow should provide the nuclei of three such institutions. But this recommendation has not been implemented; the great Imperial College continues as a constituent of London University, the Manchester College has become the University of Manchester Institute of Science and Technology, and the Glasgow College is now the University of Strathclyde.

SOME REFLECTIONS ABOUT INDEPENDENCE

There can be no doubt that public schools greatly value their independence and their admirers seem to be convinced that schools can provide a better education when free to develop as corporate societies under their own auspices. If there is any educational virtue in independence, ought we not to see that

1. Vol. I, p. 131.   2. ibid., pp. 142-3.

schools within the state system have as much of it as possible? If you read a book like E. H. Partridge's *Freedom in Education* you may wonder how anyone could nurse such dark thoughts about education under the state and local education authorities. He regarded the state control of education as 'a necessary evil', and one of his main arguments for public schools is that 'we can mitigate the evil by having at least one form of education not subject to state-control'. As for local education authorities he was quite sure that 'they cannot fairly be expected to have the necessary knowledge and experience to discharge their highly responsible task'.[1]

No one keen about state schools would resent these disparaging remarks if he had known the author of them. For, as headmaster of Giggleswick, he was a devoted schoolmaster who gave himself unsparingly to the little commonwealth over which he presided; and one can be sure that any criticism that he levelled against other ways of running schools was made with the utmost sincerity and in the belief that freedom from external control was a valuable educational asset. Nor can it be said that his views were unique: it would be more true to say that he has expressed extremely and, perhaps rashly opinions, that circulate freely in the circles in which he moved. Indeed a perusal of the relatively impartial pages of the Fleming Report will show that the public schools attribute some of their success as educational institutions to their independence, and not least to having their own governing bodies.

What the Fleming Report has to say about the governing bodies of public schools is interesting. It notes that before the passing of the Public Schools Act and the Endowed Schools Act in the eighteen-sixties the trustees or governors of these schools were often 'quite unfitted for their responsibility'. 'Hawtrey, who succeeded Keate at Eton in 1834, was continually hampered by the Provost and Fellows of Eton under the old statutes; Thring's career was marked by constant struggles with the Trustees of Uppingham.' The legislation referred to, brought important readjustments in the statutes and schemes for the governance of these schools, and gradually as the quality of

1. *Freedom in Education*, Faber, 1945, p. 88.

education improved so did that of the governing bodies. 'The prestige of the schools, the fact that they have educated a high proportion of the leading figures in the country, the loyalty of those educated at them, itself a tribute to their success, have led to the Governing bodies themselves being often composed of men of culture and ability.'[1] Is it not reasonable to hope for a similar evolution of the governing bodies of schools within the state system?

In the previous section we saw how ardently certain technical colleges sought independence, but of all our educational institutions there are none which value it so highly as do the universities. Their phrase for it is 'academic freedom' and they regard it as of paramount importance. When the Robbins Report was published discussion centred on two of its proposals: the first – soon rejected by the Government – asked for a separate Minister for Arts and Science; and the other concerned the future governance of L.E.A. training colleges. But there can be little doubt that the biggest of all the issues that confronted the Robbins Committee was the question how in the future government of the universities to combine planning with freedom. At any rate that is what seemed to them to be their major problem, as they explain when discussing it in their two chapters on 'Academic Freedom' and 'Machinery of Government'. 'We have now to approach,' they wrote, 'the most important and the most difficult of all the problems we have had to consider – what machinery of government is appropriate for a national system of higher education in this country.'[2]

The crux of this problem, as it seemed to them, was to find a proper balance 'between two necessities: the necessity of freedom for academic institutions, and the necessity that they should serve the nation's needs'.[3] So the Committee set about searching for the proper answer to the question: 'Whether it is possible for higher education to enjoy in the future at once the advantages of freedom and of orderly progress.'[4] Rather surprisingly, they came, after a careful examination of the issues involved, to the firm conclusion that their answer should be 'yes'. Their method

1. *The Public Schools and the General Educational System*, H.M.S.O., 1944, p. 44.
2. Vol. I, p. 228.   3. ibid., p. 228.   4. ibid., p. 237.

of inquiry was to study one by one various aspects of university life and practice that are traditionally free from interference: and they, at the same time, considered how these could be affected by demands that might have to be made in the national interest – whether, for example, it would be possible 'to secure the advantages of coordination, while preserving the advantages of liberty'.[1]

It is interesting to note what aspects of university affairs the Committee particularly considered because that shows what they judged to be the main constituents of academic freedom. Among them were appointments, curricula, admission of students, entrance requirements, the balance of teaching and research, freedom to develop, salaries, and staffing ratios. As they proceed with their argument, the Committee draw attention to certain limitations to institutional freedom that seem essential under modern conditions; for example, one could hardly let each university fix its own salary scale or have a widely different staffing ratio. And they observe: 'We believe that responsible academic opinion recognizes the inevitability of these limitations. There may be some who still believe that it is an outrage if the role of the State or its organs is anything but passive, but they are not many. Nevertheless the whole question of control is understandably the subject of widespread apprehension.'[2] As well as these institutional freedoms, the Committee discussed the big issue of the personal liberty of the teacher, and declared that for him 'academic freedom means the absence of discriminatory treatment on the grounds of race, sex, religion and politics: and the right to teach according to his own conception of fact and truth'.[3]

While confident that academic freedom, true to the British tradition, can be maintained the Committee were, as we have noted, very conscious of the 'widespread apprehension'. They attached the utmost importance, therefore, to the establishment of proper safeguards against possible encroachments, including those that might arise from political considerations and pressures. Exploring the ground, they focus attention on the University Grants Committee, the origins of which are referred to earlier in this chapter. 'Fortunately,' they remark, 'this country seems

1. ibid., p. 228.   2. ibid., p. 225.   3. ibid., p. 229.

to have hit upon an administrative invention that, although not precluding any such dangers, has the effect of making them much less probable – the device of interposing between the Government and institutions a committee of persons selected for their knowledge and standing and not for their political affiliation. In this way it is possible to ensure that the measures of coordination and allocation that are necessary are insulated from inappropriate political influences. This device is exemplified in the present arrangements for the famous University Grants Committee.'[1]

So they decided to recommend that this body, enlarged, strengthened and renamed the Grants Commission 'should be responsible for advising the Government on the needs of all autonomous institutions for higher education in Great Britain, and for distributing grants to them'.[2]

THE SHAPE OF THINGS TO COME

It is now possible to discern emerging through the mists of uncertainty the outlines of the new pattern of higher education. As its basis it will have the great democratic principle enunciated by the Robbins Committee – 'courses of higher education should be available for all those who are qualified by ability and attainment to pursue them and who wish to do so'.[3] Now that the Secretary of State for Education and Science has been given almost all education for his province, his influence will range far and wide affecting all our universities, colleges and schools. Clearly much will depend on the wisdom and stature of those selected for this commanding position, on their prestige in the Cabinet, and on their ability to maintain an acceptable balance of freedom and authority. It is to be hoped that the position will be regarded as of the highest importance, and not as a stepping stone. But however fortunate we may be in our Secretaries of State, the necessity for adequate counterweights will not be diminished.

The University Grants Commission will be a larger and more formidable body in the post-Robbins era, and will be

1. ibid., p. 235.   2. ibid., p. 288.   3. ibid., p. 8.

concerned with many more institutions, including new types. It will have an immensely difficult task but hopes are high that it will be able to cope with the knotty problems that will come along thick and fast as the various types of university institution expand. No doubt questions of accountability will arise as they have done in the past, and much will turn upon the degree of confidence that the Committee is able to command.

Lord Bridges spoke wisely on this theme during the House of Lords' debate on the Robbins Report.

'Given,' he said, 'the large increase in expenditure on universities, this Grants Commission will work only if the nation as a whole believes that the universities are efficiently and economically run. The Grants Commission will have to devise a system which sees that that happens and which will ensure public confidence in it. This would not be a radically new departure. In the past the University Grants Committee has, on occasion, of its own volition set on foot enquiries designed to make sure that university administration and expenditure are carried on in an economic way. All this is on the right lines; but I believe much more will have to be done in future, given the larger number and the greater variety of institutions which will now come under the guidance of the Grants Commission.'[1]

There were not more than 50,000 university students in England and Wales before the Second World War. Today there are about 216,000 students in full-time higher education, and it is proposed to increase that figure to 560,000 by 1980. By then there should be some sixty institutions of university status, including six more new universities. The large increase in the number of students will make the National Union of Students an even more important body than it is today, and there will be ample scope for wise leadership. For much will depend on the impression – or image, in current phraseology – that students make for themselves in the public mind. It will, also, give senate-student relationship a new significance; and some readers will recall that Dr Albert Sloman in his Reith Lectures devoted some time to an account of developments in this field that he hoped to see in the new University of Essex, of which he is Vice-Chancellor.

1. House of Lords, *Weekly Hansard*, No. 539, pp. 1385–6.

After noting that they were making the normal provision for student activities, he continued:

We should like to give students more say in university policy, particularly on student life, than is provided by the students' council, and better coordinate the different efforts made to provide student facilities. We propose, therefore, to set up a *student affairs committee* of the senate, headed by a dean of students, and with members drawn both from the students and from the student advisers I referred to in an earlier lecture. The student affairs committee will be responsible through the senate for all aspects of student welfare: the residential and study accommodation, provision for clubs and societies, physical education and student health. Our students will be able to make their views felt, therefore, both through their own students' council and through the student affairs committee of the senate. And the dean of students as a member of the senate by virtue of his office will represent their interests at the highest level of university policy making.[1]

Established under the aegis of the University Grants Committee, the new universities in many ways reflect U.G.C. policy. This is particularly true of their location: for the U.G.C. had firm views on this subject. They held that these new universities need not be sited like the earlier civic universities in populous areas. 'The increase in student mobility,' they claimed, 'has lessened the argument for confining the new universities to the centres of densely populated catchment areas.'[2] So they expressed a strong preference for sites of not less than 200 acres within about two or three miles of the centre of an attractive city or town. And they stressed the availability of amenities – 'good communications with other centres of learning, adequate housing at reasonable rates and the existence of good schools for children'.[3] This emphasis on amenities was due largely to their anxieties about attracting staff of good quality. 'The recruitment and retention of staff of adequate calibre may,' they urged, 'well be the limiting factor to university expansion in the next decade.'

It remains to be seen whether subsequent foundations will be

1. *Listener,* 19 December 1963, p. 1030.
2. *Returns from Universities and University Colleges, Academic Year, 1959–60,* Cmnd 1489, H.M.S.O., p. 7.
3. ibid., p. 9.

sited in such attractive surroundings as those now establishing themselves in Brighton, York, Norwich, Colchester, Canterbury, Coventry, and Lancaster. This is unlikely, for the Robbins Committee took a very different view on this question of location, urging 'the claim of the large cities and centres of population' on the ground that they offer other, more valuable advantages. Among these, says the Robbins Report, is that of convenient access to national institutions such as libraries, museums, galleries, and other cultural centres; and also to learned societies. In such areas too, the Report asserts, there is access to centres of industry, commerce, medicine, and law, to institutions of central and local government, and to research institutions. Nor do the Robbins Committee see any objection to locating more than one university in a large city; and they welcome the establishment of a second university in Glasgow as a result of the grant of a Charter to the Royal College of Science and Technology.[1]

As to the internal government of universities it seems likely that the prevailing pattern will continue – court, council, senate. There will no doubt be variations, as there are now. For example, Dr Sloman, in his Reith Lectures, had some interesting comments to make about the size of senates. Already half of them, he said, have more than 50 members, and two have 100. He anticipates that his University will eventually have 10,000 students: and observes that in a university of that size 'a senate which included all the professors and a fair representation of readers and lecturers would run to nearly 300. A body of this size would represent a ludicrously uneconomical use of some of the best brains in the country.'[2] So the aim in the University of Essex will be to have a relatively small senate – thirty at first, fifty later – composed of *ex-officio* and elected members.

Reference has already been made to the issue of lay participation in university government, and it will be remembered that the Robbins Committee strongly supported lay membership in council and court. They make a point of paying tribute to 'the initiative and wisdom of lay members on governing bodies'.[3] Much the same view was expressed by Dr Sloman in his Reith

1. Vol. I, pp. 162–3.   2. *Listener*, 19 December 1963, p. 1027.
3 Vol. I, p. 218.

Lectures and, as Vice-Chancellor of a new University, he added the further point that 'laymen have a leading part to play in integrating a university with its region'.[1] This last view was strongly held by the University Grants Committee and, when deciding their recommendations to the Government about the location of the new universities, they attached great importance to the attitude of the sponsoring groups. 'The interest of the community,' they maintained, 'is essential if a university is successfully to carry out its purposes. . . . It can only thrive in a friendly community.'[2]

Remembering ancient feuds between town and gown, it is good to note the happy relations that are being forged between the new universities and their neighbourhoods. Each in turn has been cordially welcomed: and as an illustration of this, one recalls the enthusiasm with which Lancaster greeted the Government's decision to accept the advice of the U.G.C. that a university should be established there. 'It will,' said the Mayor, 'be an exciting renaissance for Lancaster': while the Town Clerk who had played a leading part in putting forward Lancaster's claim for a university, observed: 'This marks the beginning of a new era for the city. The establishment of a university here is bound to have the deepest and most fundamental repercussions on the whole of city life.'[3]

It will certainly be interesting to see what influence the new universities have on their neighbourhoods, and no less interesting to study the effect of university expansion on society as a whole. No doubt this will at some future date be the theme of many investigations, for the big growth of universities will profoundly affect various aspects of social and economic life in this country. The Church of England has already begun to ask how it will affect its ministry. 'Our congregations,' it estimates, 'will number, if they reflect the national picture, five times as many graduates among their laity fifty years hence as they have now and far more than five times as many teachers. What should this mean for the future pattern of the ministry, ordained and lay?'[4]

1. *Listener*, 19 December 1963, p. 1027.
2. *Returns from Universities and University Colleges, Academic Year, 1959–60*, p. 8.
3. *The Times*, 24 November 1961.
4. *Report of Church of England Board of Education on Newsom and Robbins Reports*, p. 14.

Housing so many more students will be a formidable administrative problem. 'At present 28 per cent of the students in the universities, 70 per cent of students in training colleges, 22 per cent of students in Scottish colleges of education, and less than 10 per cent of students in further education are living in accommodation associated with the institutions they are attending.'[1] There is likely to be much discussion about this problem, and it may well be that 'halls of residence' will not be so readily regarded as a good solution as they are at present. Dr Sloman opened one of his Reith Lectures with the challenging statement: 'It is one of the distinctive features of the plans for the University of Essex that it will have no colleges or halls of residence. Like many Londoners and New Yorkers, our students will live in flats or apartments. . . .'[2]

In the past our schools and colleges have tended to be small: as we have already noted, until recently nearly a hundred of our training colleges had less than 250 students. Indeed, in some of our theorizing about education we used to commend the intimacy of the small community, sharing the view of William James who detested 'all big organizations'.[3] But we are getting accustomed to large numbers, and in the years ahead we must expect more and more expansion: and in our planning we shall have to provide accommodation not only for more and more staff and students but also for more and more cars. 'We decided at an early stage,' said Dr Sloman, conjuring up a vision of his university town, 'that cars would go on increasing at an alarming rate, and that students as well as staff would like to have them. Assuming that a university of 10,000 students has 15,000 people around, and that there is one car for every two of them, this means 7,500 cars, and at 175 cars to the acre there would need to be more than forty acres of car-parking.'[4] But what about England's green and pleasant land?

1. Robbins Report, Vol. I, p. 194.
2. *Listener*, 5 December 1963, p. 924.
3. Letters II, 90: quoted by Herbert Read in *Politics of the Unpolitical*, Routledge, 1943, p. 13.
4. *Listener*, 12 December 1963, p. 980.

CHAPTER 8

International Affairs

PIONEERS IN COMPARATIVE STUDIES

IT is sometimes said that our approach to education has been too 'insular', and that we have paid too little heed to what has been done in education elsewhere. It is doubtful whether this criticism is well founded: for much – perhaps, most – of our theory has come from other countries, and certainly from the earliest days of state intervention we have had administrators eager to study developments abroad. The first of our great educational administrators, Kay-Shuttleworth, set a good example in this as in other directions. Soon after his appointment in 1839 as Secretary to the Privy Council Committee on Education – our first central education department – he made a three months' tour of Europe, visiting especially Holland, France, Prussia, and Switzerland, the four countries which by that date had established state systems of education.[1]

His contacts with the Continent continued throughout his tenure of office and were a notable feature of his régime: and Dr Pollard claims, with some justice, that Kay-Shuttleworth, rather than Matthew Arnold, is entitled to be regarded as the pioneer in this country of the study of comparative education.[2] He was by no means alone in his belief that such comparative study was valuable: for, among his contemporaries, were several, including Lord Brougham, who travelled abroad to see for themselves what other countries were doing in education. But, says Dr Pollard, 'he, it must be realized, more than any man of his time, succeeded in unifying and perpetuating the ideals of a large number of those who, during the first half of the nineteenth

1. See H. M. Pollard, *Pioneers of Popular Education*, Murray, 1956, pp. 235–80.
2. ibid., pp. 246–7.

century, sought educational inspiration abroad'.[1] It is interesting
to recall that at this period another shrewd observer was studying
at first hand the educational systems of Europe – Horace Mann,
'the gifted and dynamic secretary of Massachusetts board of
education, whose career offers itself for much close comparison
with that of Kay-Shuttleworth'.[2]

Among developments in other countries that impressed Kay-
Shuttleworth was one which he usually referred to as 'Holland's
wise inspectorate'. As a good Benthamite he believed in inspection, but he had no desire to see England saddled with the
authoritarian kind of inspectorate then operating in Prussia.
The Dutch inspectors – courteous, tactful, tolerant – won his
admiration; and their example helped him to decide upon the
aims and characteristics that were, in his view, appropriate for
our inspectorate. The directions that he wrote for the guidance
of our first inspectors – H.M.I.s – have become famous and the
following extract will give some idea of their quality:

. . . It is of the utmost consequence you should bear in mind that this
inspection is not intended as a means of exercising control, but of
affording assistance; that it is not to be regarded as operating for the
restraint of local efforts, but for their encouragement; and that its chief
objects will not be attained without the cooperation of the school committees – the Inspector having no power to interfere, and not being
instructed to offer any advice or information excepting where it is
invited.

The Ministry has said that the aims of the inspectorate today
'differ hardly at all from those envisaged by Kay-Shuttleworth'.[3]
And the present Senior Chief Inspector has paid a similar tribute.
Referring to the passage in which the above extract figures, he
observes:

There is here no parsimony of imagination, no insolence or con-
descension of manner, no authoritarian tone, no dictation of detail, no
prescription of rule or method, above all no emphasis on the dead letter
of instruction or exhortation, no concern with power or conformity. The

1. ibid., p. 273.
2. Lecture by A. V. Judges on Kay-Shuttleworth in *Pioneers of English Education*,
ed. A. V. Judges, Faber, 1952, p. 117.
3. *Education in 1949*, H.M.S.O., 1950, p. 96.

whole passage is as relevant today as it was in 1840 and, had it been written today, it could hardly have been more tolerant and egalitarian in spirit, or more civilized in language. How much we all owe – in the inspectorate, and in the schools – to that wise and magnanimous man who set our course for so many years ahead . . .[1]

Of distinguished H.M.I.s none won more renown than Matthew Arnold: for he was pre-eminent, also, as a poet and man of letters, and must always rank – however much attitudes may change – as one of the greatest of the Victorian prophets. He was appointed an H.M.I. in 1851, two years after Kay-Shuttleworth had retired, and continued to hold office until 1886, two years before his death; during the greater part of his inspectorate Robert Lowe's policy of 'payments by results' was in operation. 'In defiance of official prudence Arnold exposed and condemned the Revised Code in report after report.'[2] He had a passionate belief in education, and its abuse under the Code made him angry, and all the more so because it interrupted the happy relationship between inspector and teacher that had been a cornerstone of Kay-Shuttleworth's policy.[3] It is, however, remarkable that Arnold was allowed to crusade against official policy with such candour.[4] On one occasion Sir Michael Sadler, when Director of Special Enquiries at the Board of Education, wrote anonymously to *The Times* on a question of educational policy: and, when challenged by the President admitted authorship and 'promised that he would never again send a letter on educational subjects to the Press without first showing it to the President'.[5]

Arnold is at his prophetic best in the reports that he made after official visits to the Continent in 1859 and 1865. They were written for the Newcastle and Taunton Commissions respectively: and during his 1865 tour, which occupied seven months, he made a close study of education in France, Germany, Italy,

1. Percy Wilson, *Views and Prospects from Curzon Street*, Blackwell, 1961, pp. 70–1.

2. Arnold, *Culture and Anarchy*: Dover Wilson's Introduction. Cambridge University Press, p. xiv.

3. See pamphlet on 'The Twice-Revised Code' and other articles reprinted in *Democratic Education* (Vol. II of *Complete Prose Works*) University of Michigan, 1962.

4. See Selby-Bigge, *The Board of Education*, Putnam, 1927, p. 130.

5. Lynda Grier, *Achievement in Education*, Constable, 1952, pp. 97–8.

Switzerland, and Holland. His surveys disclosed by contrast the shocking inadequacies of educational provision in England and Wales at that time, and with burning indignation Arnold pleaded for educational reform, and especially for the organization of secondary education. His reports and published articles, based on his investigations abroad, are studded with memorable passages. Sometimes they are caustic comments about official *laissez-faire*: for example, 'The State in England has shown neither taste nor aptitude for the practice of government as a profound and elaborate art; it has done what was absolutely indispensable, and has left its people to do the rest, if it could, for itself.'[1]

And, often, there are passages of scathing eloquence, of which this invocation of the 'immense working class' is a brief example:

Children of the future, whose day has not yet dawned, you, when that day arrives, will hardly believe what obstructions were long suffered to prevent its coming. You who, with all your faults, have neither the aridity of aristocracies, nor the narrow-mindedness of middle classes, you, whose power of simple enthusiasm is your great gift, will not comprehend how progress towards man's best perfection – the adorning and ennobling of his spirit – should have been for years and years retarded by barren commonplaces, by worn-out clap-traps.[2]

Thirty years passed before we reach the next great landmark in the development of comparative education in this country. In 1895 the Government decided to establish in the Education Department an 'Office of Special Enquiries and Reports' with Michael Sadler – young, dynamic, exhilarating – as its Director. It produced a number of valuable reports about aspects of education in various European countries and – a new departure – several reports on education in Commonwealth countries, e.g. Canada, Australia, New Zealand, Newfoundland, the West Indies, Ceylon, Malta. There were also two volumes on education in the U.S.A., to one of which Sadler personally contributed two articles: one being a commentary on 'Contrasts between German and American ideals in Education', while the other discussed 'The Education of the Coloured Race' in U.S.A.

1. Report on 'Popular Education in France' in *Democratic Education*.
2. Article on 'A French Eton', op cit.

Unfortunately this great enterprise encountered stormy weather and, largely as a result of quarrels with Morant, Sadler resigned in 1903. 'For a time reports continued,' Miss Grier observes in her biography of Sadler, '. . . But there have been none for many years and the Board have ceased to have a great research department.'[1] Writing in 1927, Selby-Bigge (Permanent Secretary, 1911–25) tries to put a good face on the dismal situation, noting several activities of the Board of Education in this field: but it all reads rather like a post-mortem. 'There is not now', he observes defensively, 'the same need for the same kind of official information bureau as there was thirty years ago, but in any case the limitation of the Office Staff restricts its capacity for work of the same kind and on the same scale as formerly.'[2] This sad story of how the Office of Special Enquiries and Reports waned and died provides a classic example of the harm that can ensue when top people in a Department decide to have a battle.

EXTERNAL RELATIONS

The decline and fall of the Office of Special Enquiries and Reports, as Sadler had planned it, was at the time a shattering blow: and this void in our administrative system has never since been adequately filled. It would be misleading, however, to convey the impression that, as a result, our Ministry today is out of touch with developments in other countries. It now has an efficient branch that includes 'external relations' in its province,[3] but more important is the fact that since Sadler's day there have been several new enterprises specially designed to facilitate the spread of information about educational progress in different countries and to make it easier for students, teachers, and administrators to make useful contacts with those engaged in education in other lands.

The modern world is discovering that of all human activities none offers more scope for cooperation among nations than

1. *Achievement in Education*, p. 112.
2. *The Board of Education*, pp. 215–16.
3. In 1961 a 'Research and Intelligence Branch' was established by the Ministry of Education which describes Sadler's Office in its *Annual Report* for that year (p. 126) as the new Branch's 'distinguished predecessor'.

education: and notable efforts have been made to bring their representatives together for the purpose of pooling information and promoting the advance of education. The Commonwealth is proving one of the best fields for collaboration of this kind: and much of the stimulus for joint endeavours has come from large conferences organized with great care and from a systematic follow-up of their recommendations. The first conference of this kind was held in 1907, and it was intended to arrange one every four years: but the First World War interrupted the series and, although educational conferences of Dominion representatives were held after that war, the practice of conferring in that way was abandoned during the bleak years of depression in the 1930s.

In 1959, however, this excellent habit of meeting together was revived and on a big scale. The Commonwealth Educational Conference held at Oxford in that year under the chairmanship of Sir Philip Morris was attended by some 140 delegates from all the Commonwealth countries and from 16 colonial territories. This great gathering was an outstanding success, and a further Conference was held at New Delhi three years later under the chairmanship of Dr K. C. Shrimali, Minister of Education, India. Opening the Conference the then Prime Minister, Jawaharlal Nehru, emphasized the importance of English as a medium of communication among the countries of the Commonwealth and, although the delegates were drawn from every continent, English served as a common language at all their meetings. Canada was the host of the next Conference, which is becoming a recognized institution.

Such conferences, lasting a fortnight or longer, provide valuable opportunities for informal conversations, but these Commonwealth gatherings have also been particularly successful in promoting official developments of general value. Of these a good example is the Commonwealth Scholarship and Fellowship Plan which has already done much to foster advanced studies within the Commonwealth. It is designed especially to assist men and women of high intellectual promise who have graduated and may be expected to make a significant contribution to life in their own countries on their return from study in some other Commonwealth country. The plan made an impressive start, and within two years of its initiation 650 of its scholars were studying in 14 different Commonwealth countries. The Commonwealth Bursary Scheme for Teacher Training, agreed upon at the Oxford Conference, has been no less successful and is now an established feature of Commonwealth educational cooperation. These Conferences have also led to new measures for the teaching of English as a second language: and special courses have been organized in an attempt to meet the great need for teachers of craftsmen and technicians in areas where industry is developing rapidly.

There can be no doubt that these Conferences have been remarkably successful: and there is every reason to hope that further benefits will accrue from subsequent meetings. Having said that, it may be salutary to note that large-scale conferences often miscarry. Alexander Herzen, that observant Russian democrat of the last century, remarks in his memoirs upon our addiction to them: 'Even the most serious persons,' he comments derisively, 'are sometimes overcome by the fascination of mere forms, and manage to convince themselves that they are in fact doing something if they hold meetings with a mass of documents and protocols, conferences at which facts are recorded, decisions are taken, proclamations are printed, and so forth. . . . England teems with hundreds of associations of this sort: solemn meetings take place which dukes and peers of the realm, clergymen, and secretaries, ceremoniously attend: treasurers collect funds, journalists write articles, all are busily engaged in doing nothing at all.'[1]

These Commonwealth Conferences were certainly not of the 'do nothing' kind; they have, in fact, already achieved so much – including a rich store of goodwill – that others who have to organize conferences might find it worthwhile to study their reports and try to discover the secret of their success. Much, no doubt, must be attributed to personal factors and also to a general acceptance of the fact that there is much in education that members of the Commonwealth can learn from one another. It has also, doubtless, been an advantage that the emphasis has been on action, thus diminishing opportunities for aimless debate. The purpose has been to produce definite plans for mutual

1. Quoted by Isaiah Berlin in his *Karl Marx*, Oxford University Press, 1948 ed., p. 176.

betterment, and this has given discussion a practical slant. 'A campaign,' as Macaulay well said, 'cannot be directed by a debating society.'[1]

The Conference has often broken up into groups, each entrusted with the task of studying and reporting upon specific problems. This has been an important factor in producing results: but from an administrative standpoint the two main lessons to be learnt from the story of these conferences is the crucial importance of (*a*) thorough and prolonged advance preparation, and (*b*) persistent and sustained 'following-up' of decisions arrived at.

As for 'the following-up', the Oxford Conference decided that usually schemes of educational cooperation should be carried out bilaterally, that is by contacts between two countries. But it was also agreed that some administrative organization of an intra-Commonwealth character would be necessary to assist in the development of cooperative arrangements. 'The Commonwealth Education Liaison Committee (on which the Permanent Secretary of the Ministry of Education now represents the U.K.) and the Commonwealth Education Liaison Unit were accordingly brought into existence by joint action among the governments concerned.' The Delhi Conference agreed unanimously that these administrative arrangements were working well and serving a most useful purpose: and so it was decided to continue them. And they were set an additional task. For the Delhi Conference was impressed by the growing demand for an organization which could collect information from Commonwealth countries and make it readily available to them: and the Liaison Committee was asked to assume responsibility for such a service. The Inter-University Council for Higher Education Overseas has for long done valuable work for Commonwealth cooperation in its particular sphere; and it looks as if the Commonwealth Education Liaison Unit will from its modest beginnings become a lynch-pin in the arrangements for Commonwealth cooperation in education generally.

Our concern for Commonwealth education has not diminished our interest in educational practice in other nations. We cooperate

1. See Bagehot, *Physics and Politics*, p. 192.

with other European countries through the medium of the
Council for Cultural Cooperation established by the Council of
Europe: and we participate in the business of its three permanent
committees that deal respectively with higher education and
research, general and technical education, and out-of-school
education. Under its auspices there are periodical meetings of
Ministers of Education of the member countries: they met in
Rome in 1962 and in London in 1964. We have also played an
active part in the deliberations of UNESCO since its foundation
(United Nationals Educational, Scientific and Cultural Organi-
zation) and for a number of years Sir Ben Bowen Thomas, when
Permanent Secretary of the Welsh Department of the Ministry of
Education, was Chairman of UNESCO's Executive Board.

As a source of information about educational practice in its
member states – of which there are about 120 – and as a forum for
the discussion of educational problems UNESCO has done work of
great value. It has produced many useful publications, and it
is significant of our lasting appreciation of its work that in its
annual reports our Department of Education devotes much space
to an account of UNESCO's work during the previous year. An
inevitable danger in an organization of this kind is that politics
may intrude and impair its effectiveness but, although extraneous
business will keep creeping into its deliberations, this has not
prevented much solid achievement in the field of education. 'The
Session was not without its tensions,' said our Department, sum-
marizing impressions of a controversial UNESCO conference.
'Strong feelings were aroused on a number of issues and some of
the matters raised and debated – e.g. "colonialism" – belonged to
the field of politics rather than of education, science or culture.
Nevertheless the major questions were finally settled by agreement or by decisive majorities; and there were satisfactory
indications of a general desire among member states that UNESCO
should concentrate on major lines of development of special
relevance to the developing countries.'[1] A practical comment by
our Secretary of State during his main speech to that Conference should be recorded: he said that 'he was convinced that
UNESCO would be wise to undertake the organization of fewer

1. *Education in 1962*, p. 108.

conferences so that fuller preparation for them could be made'.

But in spite of all our cooperative efforts the need for such an organization as Sadler envisaged still remains. The gap has not been filled. One is very conscious of this when reading the chapter in the Robbins Report on 'International Comparisons' and still more so when studying the volume (Appendix 5) in which is set out the information garnered by the Robbins Committee during their visits to other countries or obtained by them from Commonwealth countries that they would have liked to visit, 'if time had allowed'. It is clear that, in coming to their conclusions, the Committee found a discriminating study of these facts and figures invaluable. 'Such comparisons,' they observe, 'are full of pitfalls . . . but to look at systems very different in structure brings into the open assumptions implicit in the British pattern. Our experiences abroad have confirmed some cherished beliefs about the excellence of British higher education, but they have caused us to re-examine others. Moreover, if proper precautions are taken, it is possible to compare quantitatively the provision made here with that overseas, and this has led us seriously to question the adequacy of what is at present planned in this country.'[1] We owe much to our leading exponents of comparative education and to our educational press, but they, those set in authority over education, and many intelligent citizens would greatly benefit if we now had the kind of bureau that might have evolved but for the tragic Sadler–Morant affair.

STUDENTS FROM OVERSEAS

Wandering scholars in search of knowledge are as much a feature of the twentieth as they were of the twelfth century. Our own scholars go abroad to pursue their studies, but many more come to our shores to continue their education. Our universities are by no means the only magnet: about as many attend technical colleges, and others come as student nurses (about 6,000), for industrial, commercial, and practical training, or as prospective barristers to attend the Inns of Court (about 2,000), and a growing number come to train as teachers. In 1961–2 about 10 per cent of

1. Vol. I, p. 35.

all full-time students in higher education came from abroad. About 7 per cent of the undergraduates in our universities were overseas students, and so were 32 per cent of the postgraduates. In further education 15 per cent were from overseas, and they number about 2 per cent of students preparing to become teachers.[1] About 60 per cent of these overseas students came here from Commonwealth countries: over 1,000 from the U.S.A. and among other countries that send us a good many students are France, Germany, Norway, and Iraq. Some come for industrial training, and that enlightened firm, long known as Metropolitan Vickers, has trained more than 4,000 overseas apprentices in the past few decades.[2]

A great many of these students come from developing countries in Africa and Asia, and sometimes find it difficult to adapt themselves to their new surroundings. It is important to make them feel welcome, to provide courses of study or training that meet their requirements, and to ensure, as far as possible, that they are comfortably housed and have the sort of meals that they like. A great deal is being done by universities, technical colleges, training colleges, government departments, the British Council, the Churches, and several organizations; but with the growing numbers and the increasing diversity of our visitors the problems multiply. Now that education has an overlord, one would like to think that somewhere in his large domain there will be a high-powered but very accessible officer who has the well-being of all overseas students as his special responsibility.

Much has already been done to provide hostel accommodation, but clearly more is needed and, as a P.E.P. report suggests, there is a preference for hostels shared with British students. 'The combination of a threadbare lodging house and the grey pall of an English winter,' says Mr Livingstone in his interesting study of *The Overseas Student in Britain*, 'can daunt the most exuberant spirit from overseas. It would be unfair to attribute culpability for this to landladies who, in many individual cases, have tried hard to provide a congenial atmosphere for their overseas guests. But

---

1. Robbins Report, Vol. I, p. 15.
2. A. S. Livingstone, *The Overseas Student in Britain*, Manchester University Press, 1960, p. 20.

you cannot take people away from a sun-soaked land, with all its associations of food, fun, and deep family ties, and expect them to feel at ease in the bleak isolation of a lodging house.'[1]

While there are certainly serious difficulties about accommodation, the general picture is far from gloomy. In universities, colleges, and other institutions throughout the country the overseas students are made very welcome: and when they return to their homeland, they take with them, with rare exceptions, warm feelings of regard for Britain and her people. Many of them are potential leaders, and it is significant that no less than 5,400 of the 14,900 postgraduate students (excluding those studying education) in our universities come from overseas. Of these 3,800 are engaged in research, and 1,600 are following courses of study. There are, too, another 720 postgraduate overseas students among the 4,500 students in our university education departments.[2]

The benefit reaped in the diffusion of goodwill must be considerable but, like most of the good things in education, it cannot be measured. The story of the Rhodes Trust provides an illustration of the good that can accrue when, year after year, students from other countries are made welcome and given the best that a university has to offer. When the Trust celebrated its jubilee in 1953, nearly 3,000 Rhodes Scholars had passed through Oxford during the half century. Some had attained high distinction – there were among them Prime Ministers, an O.M., a Nobel Prizeman, and several other notabilities – but the great majority, while they had done well, were not in exalted positions, though many were outstanding in their different vocations, especially in teaching, the law, and journalism.[3]

'I have no doubt,' wrote Lord Elton at the time of this jubilee, 'that that familiar but shadowy figure, the future historian, will in due course recognize and record the far-reaching aggregate impact of successive generations of Rhodes Scholars, not only upon their native countries, but upon the Commonwealth as a whole and upon the relations, both collectively of the Commonwealth, and

1. pp. 6 and 7.
2. See Robbins Report, pp. 98, 99.
3. Some of the narrative in this section is taken from an article by the author on 'Students from Overseas' in *The Municipal Review*, May 1961.

individually of its members, with Great Britain and the United States.'[1] The success of the Rhodes Trust has led to the establishment of several other foundations with similar objectives, and among them the well-known system of scholarships in the U.S.A. associated with the name of Senator Fulbright, himself a former Rhodes Scholar. 'My experience as a Rhodes Scholar,' he once wrote, 'was the dominant influence in the creation of the Fulbright awards.'[2]

Lord Elton's comment, quoted above, is broadly applicable to ex-students from overseas generally. Collectively, and sometimes as individuals, they exercise an immense influence. We can expect during the coming years many more student visitors and there will be more of our own students going abroad to pursue their studies and widen their outlook – a two-way movement which, adequately encouraged, can do much to promote international understanding and goodwill.

ATTITUDES TO EDUCATION

In shaping educational policy, governments are actuated by different motives. Here, as the Crowther Committee suggest, we tend to see education both as a national investment and as a human right. We soon find that we cannot consider policy under either of these headings without reference to the educational situation in other countries. The White Paper on Technical Education, which in 1956 initiated a new policy in that branch of the service, provides a good illustration not only of the national investment outlook, but also of the use of comparative data to justify action. It opens dramatically with a reference to developments overseas. 'From the U.S.A., Russia, and Western Europe,' it observes, 'comes the challenge to look to our system of technical education to see whether it bears comparison with what is being done abroad.' And it buttresses its case for immediate expansion with an appendix of facts and figures under the heading 'Note on the U.S.A., U.S.S.R. and Western Europe'.

When human right is the keynote of our policy, our first aim is

---

1. *The Rhodes Trust, 1903–53*, Blackwell, 1955, p. 54.
2. op. cit., p. 212.

to ensure that our children have a square deal over their schooling and that their opportunities are at least as good as those in other countries with an established educational system. And, if we discharge our 'human rights' obligation conscientiously, we bear in mind the education clauses in the Declaration of Human Rights passed and proclaimed by General Assembly of the United Nations in 1948. Among its provisions is one that declares that 'Everyone has the right to education' and another that demands that education 'shall promote understanding, tolerance, and friendship among all nations'. The member states were asked to arrange for the Declaration 'to be disseminated, displayed, read and expounded principally in schools and other educational institutions'. How far this is being done, one cannot say. But there can be few people who have visited more schools in England than Dr A. G. Hughes, formerly Chief Inspector of Schools for the London County Council: and it is significant that in a book, written in collaboration with his wife in which he garners impressions based on the experience of a life-time, this Declaration is printed in full with a comment that it 'is informed by many of the same ideas as those expounded in this book'. There is an interesting comment, too, on the cumulative effect of lessons given in schools throughout the world based on this Declaration which shows the value that the authors place on teaching of this kind. 'A teacher's influence,' they suggest, 'should thus be thought of as one that may spread in widening circles in space and time: beginning now as an influence on the growth of individuals in his class-room, it may end in time as an influence on the growth of partnership on a world-wide scale.'[1]

Alas, the cold war is still a determinant of educational policy in many countries. There is heavy expenditure on defence, and funds that might otherwise be devoted to education and other social services have to be spent on armaments. In such circumstances education acquires a military significance and like Milton, in the turbulent seventeenth century, we think of it as a preparation 'for the offices, both private and public, of peace and war'. Our rulers look to education to provide the adaptable personnel that modern

1. A. G. and E. H. Hughes, *Education: Some Fundamental Problems*, Longmans, 1959, pp. 285–6.

war requires, including highly intelligent scientific and technological experts. It is also a regrettable fact that the cold war not
only diverts education from its better purposes in the established
countries, but it is also a disturbing factor in the educational life
of some of the emergent nations.

THE IMPACT OF NATIONALITY ON EDUCATION

What is a Nation? There is no satisfying definition and those who
insist upon one must be reminded of George Meredith's wise
words:

> Ah what a dusty answer gets the soul
> When hot for certainties in this our life.

After considering various well-known attempts at a definition
Ernest Barker suggested a comprehensive one which, although a
masterly effort, will not any more than the others win unanimous
approval. While likely, for example, to find some warm critics in
Wales and Scotland, it is probably as good an answer to this
question as we are likely to get. 'Shall we say,' he wrote, 'that a
nation is a body of men, inhabiting a definite territory, who
normally are drawn from different races, but possess a common
stock of thoughts and feelings acquired and transmitted during
the course of a common history; who on the whole and in the
main, though more in the past than in the present, include in that
common stock a common religious belief; who generally and as a
rule use a common language as the vehicle of their thoughts and
feelings; and who, besides thoughts and feelings also cherish a
common will, and accordingly form, or tend to form, a separate
state for the expression of that will.'[1]

The medieval universities forged the first link between education and nations: for, receiving students from many countries, it
was natural for the masters and students to divide themselves into
'nations' much as schools today are often organized as 'houses'.
But nation-states had not come into existence at that time nor had
'nations' as we conceive them. Indeed in England the two

1. *National Character*, Methuen, 1927, p. 17.

universities did not organize themselves as 'nations': they divided into northerners and southerners – Boreales and Australes – using the River Trent as the dividing line. It is not until the latter part of the eighteenth century that we get a revival of the Greek idea of education as an auxiliary of the state. Montesquieu, for example, in his famous *Esprit des Lois* (1748) maintains, just as Aristotle did, that the educational system ought to reflect a country's principles of government.

It is important to remember that there are different kinds of nationality, and there are today two main types that bear little or no resemblance to each other. One is essentially social, expressing itself usually in common thoughts and feelings, religion, language, literature, music, customs, and dress. A nation of this kind, especially if it conducts its affairs in a friendly, unaggressive spirit, can by developing and encouraging its own culture and literature enrich and enliven education. At the other extreme is the forceful, militaristic nation, organized as a state and ready not only to defend its own interests but also to expand its sphere of influence. It is usually enthusiastic in its support of its particular culture and education, but expects its schools and youth organizations to foster an intense patriotism and promote those Spartan qualities that make brave soldiers.

Let us first consider the predominantly social type. There is much to be said for the multi-national state in which nations of this kind co-exist; and as regards education, there is value in the diversity – one of the principal characteristics of such a state – for it is a valuable preventive of excessive centralization. Inevitably it has its problems and they can be seen in full measure in a country like Belgium which has to cope with so many tensions – Catholics and Liberals, Flemings and Walloons, and the controversies of rival communes. 'It has,' says Professor Mallinson in his fascinating study of Belgian education, 'language problems, it has political problems, it has religious problems, yet it is a thriving community of people strongly resisting centralization or bureaucratic control of any kind and who, in adversity, manifest the most determined patriotism.'[1]

1. Vernon Mallinson, *Power and Politics in Belgian Education, 1815–1961*, Heinemann, 1963, p. x.

In our country we encourage diversity and respect national traditions. Although England and Scotland have shared one parliament since the Union in 1707, the Scots have fully maintained their separate and distinctive educational system, for which three centuries ago John Knox and his followers set the general pattern. It differs from that in England in many respects, especially, as noted in an earlier chapter, by its avoidance of a dual system. Parliament legislates for Scottish education separately, and the various enactments were recently consolidated in the Education (Scotland) Act, 1962.

The Secretary of State for Scotland is responsible to Parliament for the general control and direction of the educational system, and there is a separate Education Office in St Andrew's House, Edinburgh. A liaison staff is maintained in London for contact with Parliament and other government departments. Scotland has its own Advisory Council for education, now constituted under clause 73 of the 1962 Act. Education is administered locally by the county councils and the councils of the large burghs. Northern Ireland, self-governing since 1921, has its own Parliament and its own Ministry of Education: and under its Education Act of 1923 each county and county borough was constituted the local education authority for its area. It has its own Association of Education Committees which is in close touch with the A.E.C. for England and Wales, the Director of Education for Belfast being a coopted member of the latter's Executive Committee.

Education acts applicable to England apply also to Wales. But there is within the Department of Education a Secretary for Welsh Education, an Education Office for Wales in Cardiff, and a Welsh Inspectorate. While its educational system is the same as that of England, it has a distinctive educational tradition and a vigorous national culture in which religion, music, drama, and literature figure prominently. For over 30 per cent of the children Welsh is the language of the home and much thought has been given by the Advisory Council for Education (Wales), the university education departments, the training colleges, and the Welsh Joint Education Committee to the teaching of Welsh. The demand for Welsh children to be taught in their native tongue has a long history, dating at least to the beginnings of the S.P.C.K. (1699) and the early charity schools.[1] But until late in the nineteenth century it was the practice of English administrators to frown upon the use of Welsh in school, and a misguided Commission set up in 1846 to report on education in Wales gave this derogatory attitude every encouragement. One even finds Matthew Arnold, when an H.M.I., writing: 'The sooner the Welsh language disappears, as an instrument of the practical, social life of Wales, the better.'[2]

Towards the close of the nineteenth century Parliament's attitude to Welsh aspirations began to change. In 1889 the Welsh Intermediate Education Act was passed; in 1893 the Welsh university colleges were incorporated federally in a University of Wales; and in 1907 the separate Welsh department was created within the Board of Education. There followed a complete reversal of the traditional policy of disparaging the Welsh language, and in the White Paper that prepared the way for the 1944 Education Act special consideration was given to education in Wales. 'The policy of the Board,' it observed penitently, 'has now been officially disassociated from the views about the Welsh language expressed by the Commission of Inquiry in 1846.' And it continued with this wise, cautionary comment: 'It is now hoped that the encouragement of studies which are traditional to Wales will not be developed so as to form a barrier between Wales and its neighbours but will provide a livelier association in the world of thought and culture.'[3]

Let us now look briefly at the militant type of nationality and its significance for education. Nations in Europe began to be conscious of their nationality early in the nineteenth century: but before then influences had been at work – for example, the partition of Poland, 'the first destruction of a nation' – that had kindled the flame of nationalism. 'In the world of action,' writes Ernest Barker, 'apprehended ideas are alone electrical: and a nation must be an idea as well as a fact before it can become a dynamic force. . . . The nations became aware of nationality and nationalism became the apprehended idea of their lives.'[4] The

---

1. See Dr Mary Clement's *The S.P.C.K. in Wales*, S.P.C.K., 1954. Welsh readers will find a good account of continuous pressure for teaching in Welsh in W. R. Jones's *Addysg Ddwyieithog Yng Nghymru*, Caernarvon, 1963.

2. *Celtic Literature*, Smith, Elder, 1891 ed., p. 10.

3. *Educational Reconstruction*, p. 31. 4. *National Character*, pp. 123–4.

French Revolution hastened the growth of the idea: for it demonstrated what immense power the collective energy of a great nation can generate when it is emotionally aroused.

Napoleon, though an empire-builder, believed in nations and especially in his beloved France. In shaping her reconstruction he soon realized the political significance of education. 'There will be no fixed political state,' he declared, 'if there is no teaching body with fixed principles. As long as children are not taught whether they ought to be republican or monarchical, Catholic or irreligious, the State cannot properly be called a Nation.' 'He was resolved,' says H. A. L. Fisher, 'that young France should be schooled in the military, religious, and deferential temper, after the Spartan or Jesuit example.'[1]

But, as noted in Chapters 1 and 2, it was not what Napoleon did in France but his great victory at Jena that created the situation that led to the birth of the movement in which education became an instrument of militant nationalism. The situation was one of tragic humiliation for Prussia but her leaders at once set to work to achieve a regeneration and were busy with their plans for the future while French garrisons were still in occupation. Such determination was beyond praise, nor could it be said that those who were in charge of educational reform at that initial period were militant or illiberal. Von Humboldt who first had charge of educational reconstruction was, as we have already observed, a distinguished scholar with generous ideals and a love of Greek thought and literature. J. S. Mill, the arch-prophet of Victorian Liberalism, quotes with warm approval von Humboldt's belief in the encouragement of 'individual vigour and manifold diversity'.[2]

But there were other voices, notably that of the philosopher J. G. Fichte, who courageously delivered his famous *Addresses to the German People* while the French were still in occupation. He called upon his countrymen to work for the revival of their Fatherland and the creation of a united Germany: and for this stupendous task he cast education in the principal role. Its supreme task was to mould the patriotic citizen and make him as

1. *Napoleon*, Oxford University Press (Home University Library), pp. 157–8.
2. Essay *On Liberty*, Watts (Thinkers' Library), 1929 ed., p. 69.

ready and able as the Spartans of old to serve the fatherland. To achieve that, Fichte urged, 'you must fashion him, and fashion him, and fashion him in such a way that he simply cannot will otherwise than you wish him to will'. 'This is why,' comments Professor Kedourie in his study of *Nationalism*, 'on nationalist theory, education must have a central position in the work of the state. The purpose of education is not to transmit knowledge, traditional wisdom, and the ways devised by a society for attending to the common concerns; its purpose rather is wholly political, to bend the will of the young to the will of the nation. Schools are instruments of state policy, like the army, the police, and the exchequer.'[1]

The schools performed their task well and, after the triumph of the German armies and the French surrender at Sedan (1870), the state schools of Germany were renowned throughout the world for their enterprise and efficiency as were its universities for their sound learning. Education helped the Germany of the Hohenzollerns to become a powerful industrial empire and prepared its armies for the First World War, and then in the hands of Hitler and his entourage all the worst attributes of an intensely nationalist education were nakedly revealed. At Versailles (1919), after the First World War, the doctrine of self-determination led to the creation of more nations and there have been some important additions since. 'But,' writes Professor Kedourie sadly, 'the attempt to re-fashion so much of the world on nationalist lines has not led to greater peace and stability.'[2]

THE GREAT AWAKENING

It is idle to speculate about the future: who, for example, a century ago would have been believed if he had foretold the two world wars, the dominance of the U.S.A. and the U.S.S.R., and China's present position in the world. But it does look as if a hundred years on some of the new nations developing today will by then be a powerful influence in the world. Destiny is no artist, and it is unlikely that their growth will happen according to plan

1. E. Kedourie, *Nationalism*, Hutchinson, 1961 ed., pp. 83–4.
2. ibid., p. 138.

or that the pattern that seems to be emerging will survive. But it is a movement of such potential significance that it may well prove in its consequences to be the greatest happening of this century. Dr Gunnar Myrdal the eminent Swedish economist has coined a splendid phrase to describe this dynamic rush towards national independence and economic development. He has called it 'the Great Awakening': and Dr Adam Curle in his inaugural lecture as Professor of Education in the University of Ghana, made the further point that 'among the economically established nations, too, there has been an awakening of awareness, of conscience even, that so many peoples of the world are still suffering the direst effects of poverty'.[1]

We in this country are closely concerned with these developments because of our long association with some of the new nations. We have, as our historians like to remind us, had our own difficulties in building up our curious educational system, but they were as nothing when compared with those now confronting some of the nations that have in recent years become self-governing. They are face to face with a cruel dilemma: how to meet the intense demand for education with an inadequate economy, and how to develop that economy without an educational system able to supply the necessary educated personnel.[2] The problems must, on the spot, frequently seem insoluble, but they are being tackled courageously: and often with that kind of desperate faith which sustains administrators in dark moments and helps them to believe that

Even the weariest river winds somewhere safe to sea.

Material development is vital to the education of all nations, young and old: and that is largely why an organization like UNESCO lays stress on social services and food production and why we have our own admirable Ministry of Overseas Development. It is good to see that when new nations, with which we have been associated, become self-governing our educational

1. *The Role of Education in Developing Societies*, Ghana University Press, 1961, p. 5.
2. For a stimulating and informative survey of problems confronting some of the new nations, see W. E. F. Ward's *Educating Young Nations*, Allen and Unwin, 1959, with a Foreword by H. L. Elvin.

relationship with them does not cease. On the contrary, there is emerging a new kind of educational partnership which, adequately encouraged, could become an important stabilizing influence in our unsettled world. If cooperation in education among the nations grows in strength, as well it may, Dr Arnold Toynbee's noble vision of a united world in the twenty-first century will become more and more credible, and it will then not be difficult to share his belief that in religion sectarianism will give way to unity and that in politics nationalism will be subordinated to world government.

Books for Further Reading

MAINLY HISTORICAL

Barnard, H. C. A., *A Short History of English Education, 1760–1944*, University of London Press, 1947.

Beales, A. C. F., *Education under Penalty: English Catholic Education from the Reformation to the Fall of James II*, Athlone Press, 1963.

Boyd, W., *History of Western Education*, A. & C. Black, 7th ed., 1964, revised by E. J. King.

Castle, E. B., *Ancient Education and Today*, Penguin Books, 1961.

Cruickshank, M., *Church and State in English Education: 1870 to the Present Day*, Macmillan, 1963.

Curtis, S. J., *History of Education in Great Britain*, University Tutorial Press, 6th ed., 1965.

Dent, H. C., *Education in Transition*, Routledge & Kegan Paul, 5th ed., 1948.

Gwynn, A., *Roman Education from Cicero to Quintilian*, Clarendon Press, 1926.

Jarman, T. L., *Landmarks in the History of Education*, Cresset Press, 1951.

Leeson, Spencer, *Christian Education*, Longmans, 1947.

Lowndes, G. A. N., *The Silent Social Revolution*, Oxford University Press, 2nd ed., 1948.

Myers, Edward D., *Education in the Perspective of History*, New York, Harper, 1960.

Payne, E. A., *The Free Church Tradition in the Life of England*, S.C.M. Press, 1944.

Simon, Brian, *Studies in the History of Education*, Vol. I, 1780–1870, Vol. II, 1870–1920, Lawrence & Wishart, 1960, 1965.

Trevelyan, G. M., *English Social History*, Longmans, 1944.

MAINLY POLITICAL

Barker, Ernest, *Reflections on Government*, O.U.P., 1942.

Barker, Ernest, *National Character*, Methuen, 1927.

Finer, H., *English Local Government*, Methuen, 4th ed., 1950.

Harrison, W., *The Government of Britain*, Hutchinson, 4th ed., 1957.

Jennings, Sir I., *The Queen's Government*, Penguin Books, 1954.

Jouvenel, B. de, *Power: the Natural History of its Growth*, Batchworth Press, revised ed., 1952.

Kedourie, E., *Nationalism*, Hutchinson, revised ed., 1961.

Robson, W. A., and others, *British Government since 1918*, Allen & Unwin, 1950.

Russell, Bertrand (Lord Russell), *Power*, Allen & Unwin, 1938.

Wheare, K. C., *Government by Committee*, Oxford University Press, 1955.

Wootton, B. (Lady Wootton of Abinger), *Freedom under Planning*, Allen & Unwin, 1945.

MAINLY SOCIOLOGICAL

Banks, O., *Parity and Prestige in English Secondary Education*, Routledge & Kegan Paul, 1955.

Blyth, W. A. L., *English Primary Education*, Vols. I and II, Routledge & Kegan Paul, 1965.

Garforth, F. W., *Education and Social Purpose*, Oldbourne, 1962.

King, R., *Education*, Longmans, 1969.

Mays, J. B., *Education and the Urban Child*, Liverpool University Press, 1962.

Mannheim, K., *Diagnosis of our Time*, Routledge & Kegan Paul, 1940.

Musgrave, P. W., *The Sociology of Education*, Methuen, 1965.

Ottaway, A. K. C., *Education and Society: an Introduction to the Sociology of Education*, Routledge & Kegan Paul, 2nd ed., 1962.

MAINLY ABOUT THE ADMINISTRATION OF EDUCATION

Alexander, Sir W., *Education in England. The National System – How it Works*, Newnes, 2nd ed., 1964.

Baron, G., *A Bibliographical Guide to the English Education System*, 3rd ed., Athlone Press, 1965.

Dent, H. C., *The Educational System of England and Wales*, University of London Press, 4th ed., 1969.

Dunsire, A., and others, *The Making of an Administrator*, Manchester University Press, 1956.

Mountford, Sir J., *British Universities*, Oxford University Press, 1966.

Scottish Education Dept., *Public Education in Scotland*, Edinburgh, H.M.S.O., 1955.

Vaizey, J., *The Costs of Education*, Allen & Unwin, 1958.

Books for Further Reading

Vaizey, J., *Education for Tomorrow*, Penguin Books, 1962.

Venables, Sir P., *Technical Education: its Aims, Organization, and Future Development*, Bell, 1955.

MAINLY ABOUT THE EDUCATION OF AN ÉLITE

Bamford, T. W., *Rise of the Public Schools*, Nelson, 1967.

Brogan, Sir D., *The English People* (especially Chapter 2), Hamish Hamilton, 1943.

Crossman, R. H., *Plato Today*, Allen & Unwin (Unwin Books ed.), 1963.

Higher Education (Report of the Committee of Higher Education. Chairman: Lord Robbins), Cmnd. 2154, H.M.S.O., 1963.

James, E. (Lord James of Rusholme), *Education and Democratic Leadership*, Harrap, 1951.

Plato, *The Republic*, translated by H. D. P. Lee, Penguin Books, 1955.

Young, Michael, *The Rise of the Meritocracy*, Penguin Books, 1961.

MAINLY ABOUT EDUCATION IN OTHER COUNTRIES

Arnold, Matthew, *Democratic Education* (Vol. II of *Complete Prose Works of Matthew Arnold*), edited by R. H. Super, Michigan, University of Michigan, 1962.

Grant, N., *Soviet Education*, Penguin Books, revised ed., 1968.

Hans, N., *Comparative Education*, Routledge & Kegan Paul, 1949.

Kandel, I. L., *The New Era in Education*, Harrap, 1955.

King, E. J., *Other Schools and Ours*, New York, Rinehart, 1958.

Richmond, W. K., *Education in the U.S.A.*, Alvin Redman, 1956.

Ward, W. E. F., *Educating Young Nations*, Allen & Unwin, 1959.

Index

Another Pelican by W. O. Lester Smith

EDUCATION

AN INTRODUCTORY SURVEY

Intended for the general reader, this book attempts to provide an account of modern trends in educational theory and practice, and it reviews current problems.

It presents for the reader's consideration most of the fundamental issues under discussion today in educational circles – aims and principles, the interaction of home and school, the curriculum, the significance of the neighbourhood, problems of control and administration, equality of opportunity, the education and status of teachers, the organization of secondary education, the influence of the Churches and voluntary societies, and the educational needs of an industrial society.

A brief survey of this kind can be a dreary catalogue if it is not selective, and for that reason there are some important omissions. It has been assumed that many readers will wish to study more closely aspects and issues that particularly interest them, and throughout there are references to relevant literature, including many books to which the author is specially indebted. A reading list has also been appended in the hope that it will prove helpful. Several revisions have been made in this reprint, to bring the book up to date.

'Cool, unbiased, objective, tolerant' *The Times Educational Supplement*